MW01279875

'In Spirit and
in Truth'

Translated from the French
Original title: 'EN ESPRIT ET EN VÉRITÉ'

Omraam Mikhaël Aïvanhov

'In Spirit and in Truth'

2ⁿᵈ edition

Izvor Collection — No. 235

PROSVETA

Prosveta S.A – B.P.12 – 83601 Fréjus CEDEX (France)

ISSN 0763-2738
ISBN 2-85566-704-6
1ère édition: ISBN 1-895978-06-8 (Canada)
édition originale: ISBN 2-85566-566-3

TABLE OF CONTENTS

Chapter One

THE FRAMEWORK OF THE UNIVERSE

Initiatic science has always drawn an analogy between the universe—the macrocosm, and a human being—the microcosm.

Imagine how puzzling it would be for someone who, knowing nothing of human anatomy or of the structure that lies under the skin, tried to understand what holds people together; what keeps them upright and makes them capable of walking, breathing and eating, what enables them to express thoughts and feelings. You would have to explain to him that hidden by the skin there is a framework of bones to which are attached flesh, muscles, organs, blood, and nerves. Well, this is also true, on a gigantic scale, of the universe itself. The universe is a body, the body of God. And our own physical bodies are created in its image. Just as our bodies are built on the framework of a skeleton—without which they would collapse—the universe itself hangs on a framework thanks to which all its constituent parts, from the galaxies to the minute particles of matter that make up the atoms, are held together in equilibrium. It is this framework that we call the world of principles. It is this framework that makes life possible.

If you want to understand how the universe is built and how it functions you have to be able to see the whole skeleton of this cosmic body, from head to toe. For years and years this is what I endeavoured to do. Through meditation and contemplation, I did my best to discover the laws that governed the construction of the universe. Through dissociation[1] I would rise to the highest peak from which the whole edifice can be seen. Obviously no human being can ever quite manage to see creation as the Creator sees it, but at least we can try to get as close to his point of view as possible. And the only way to do this is to free oneself from the material density and limitations of earth. For truth, first and foremost, is a point of view, and we can only acquire this point of view by distancing ourselves from the world that is constantly before our eyes.

[1] Dissociation, an altered state of consciousness in which one is no longer aware of one's physical environment, sometimes called astral projection .

If you have never thought about any of this, of course, it may be difficult for you to see what I mean when I speak of seeing the universe from a distance. It might help you to understand this better if I compare the experience with that of astronauts in outer space: they see the earth and the rest of the universe from a quite different point of view. Every human being possesses within himself the equivalent of the spaceship that carries astronauts into space. The Creator has given each one of us centres and subtle bodies that enable us to make contact with spiritual realities in the same way as our five senses enable us to make contact with the realities of the physical world.

You will know truth when you are able to embrace the gigantic edifice of creation, from the summit to the base, in one glance. In the normal way we see the world as a heterogeneous collection of unrelated creatures, elements, objects and phenomena. The truth is that there is order in this diversity, and all the different elements are interrelated, but the intellect is incapable of grasping the overall reality. This is why it is impossible for me to show you the totality all at once. In each talk I can give you a glimpse of no more than a small part of the whole. Each talk is just one element of the whole vast structure. One day, when you succeed through your own inner work in putting all these elements together, you

will suddenly find that you are able to grasp the
unity of the world. I can explain no more than that.

In any case, there are certain questions that all
initiates prefer to pass over in silence, for try as
they might it is simply not possible to explain them
by objective, intellectual reasoning. The only truly
effective way of getting their disciples to
understand would be to take them back to a
primordial state of consciousness in which
everything is understood without explanations. To
attempt anything else is like trying to get a blind
person to understand the colours of a sunrise, or a
deaf person to appreciate a Mass by Mozart or
Beethoven. Explanations are useless. But give them
back their sight or their hearing and all
explanations become superfluous.

When the first human beings dwelt in the
bosom of their heavenly Father they were in
constant communion with him, and had access to
all knowledge. The divine life in which they were
immersed was their unique and peerless source of
information. To know something is to taste it, to
savour it. If you want to recapture something of
that primordial knowledge you must be in
communion with the whole universe, with the
ocean of cosmic light. As long as you fail to reach
the state of consciousness known as communion,
you cannot know reality, because you cannot
savour it. You can formulate any number of

suppositions and theories which may come fairly close to the truth, but they will never be more than an approximation.

'So what is the use of explanations?' you ask. The use of explanations is that they stimulate your curiosity, they trigger in you the desire to exert yourselves in certain ways, to experience things for yourselves, to become capable of living in an altered state of consciousness. All that I have been saying to you for years comes from the vision that I have been granted of the sublime order that governs the universe. I give you the elements and point you in the right direction, and if you know how to work, you too will be given this vision of truth.

Chapter Two

THE DIVINE OFFICE
OF WEIGHTS AND MEASURES

According to the philosophy of the initiates there is one unique and eternal truth. This means that all the beliefs and opinions held by human beings can be considered true only to the extent to which they come close to this one, eternal principle, which is the heart of all reality. Until such time as you reach this heart the truth you hold is simply your truth and nothing more. All that you believe to be true is, of course, a form of truth, but only a relative form. You say, 'To my mind things are thus and so…' and perhaps in saying this you imagine that you are identifying with truth. But what may seem self-evident to you is not necessarily the truth. There are two different realities involved here: yourself and the truth. What makes you think that your truth is universal truth? If you could test this assumption you would be obliged to see how far off the mark you are.

There can be no absolute definition of truth, for human beings change and their definitions change with them. You have all been children. You have all played with toys, and know that if you broke a favourite toy or someone took it away from you, it was a veritable tragedy. If you tell a child that some things are more important than its dolls, or toy soldiers, or miniature cars, it will not believe you. These things are a child's whole world. They are his truth. But adolescents laugh at the things they found important as children. They will say that they used to be very naïve, because now their truth is elsewhere, it is in their friends, their success in the classroom, and so on. But only a few years hence they and their truths will have changed again. Is there anything wrong with this? No, not at all. It is perfectly normal for human beings to progress in this way. But what is important is that they should constantly progress towards higher truths, that they should constantly reach a higher level of understanding, and a broader point of view, so that at the age of ninety they no longer make do with the truths that satisfied them at the age of fifteen.

It is relatively easy to explain why human beings hold certain opinions or behave in certain ways. It is easy also to understand that they are liable to make many mistakes and do many stupid things. Yes, we can understand this, but to claim that their thoughts and behaviour conform strictly to the truth is quite another matter. Individuals judge according to their own faculties, abilities, temperament, and needs. That is all. And yet with what arrogance they declare that they believe or do not believe something, as though they were proclaiming an eternal truth! As though it had to be true or untrue just because they believed or refused to believe! But it is not a question of believing or not believing, it is a question of studying and verifying things for oneself. Only in this way can you come close to truth. Do those who declare that they believe know why they believe? What is the source of their belief? Human beings believe a great many things because it suits them, because it is to their advantage to do so. They believe what corresponds to their needs and their sensibilities. Well, they are fully within their rights to believe whatever they like, but they should not think that what they believe is necessarily the truth. Above all they should never try to force their beliefs on others.

One sometimes hears people expressing admiration for a man who has strong convictions and who defends them openly. They think that it is magnificent to be ready to fight for one's convictions. Of course, there is nothing reprehensible in having convictions. No one can live without them. What is reprehensible is never to examine the basis of one's convictions, never to wonder whether they should not be revised occasionally. From the viewpoint of wisdom, the attitude of some of those who hold strong convictions is rather one of pride or stupidity, and the consequences can be terrible fanaticism and cruelty.

I strongly advise you to stop declaring that you believe or do not believe, for your beliefs cannot alter reality. The only thing you need to be concerned about is whether or not your beliefs make you better, stronger, more generous and more understanding of others. If they do not then you have nothing to be proud of.

A wise man will say, 'Who am I to lay down the law? When I think of all the blunders I have made, and all the harm I have already done, all the failures and disappointments I have met with, how can I be sure that my opinions are right?'

If you want to perceive things clearly and reason correctly on the basis of that perception, you must have the necessary instruments. And they must be in good working order. What instruments am I talking about? The intellect, the heart, and the will. Unfortunately, we are forced to recognize that in most human beings these instruments are faulty. Their intellects have been clouded, their hearts numbed, and their wills weakened by too many shocks, too much nervous tension and emotion, too many negative influences. How can anyone hope to perceive truth with the help of such instruments? It is obvious that they need to be checked and adjusted.

Human beings know that it is indispensable to have certain fixed norms and standards on the physical plane. For instance, the French National Office of Weights and Measures kept its standards and instruments of calibration here in Sèvres for years, and they served as a frame of reference for the whole world. Standards are always necessary. What unspeakable confusion would reign if each individual calculated the length of a metre or the weight of a kilogram to suit himself! Even the length of hours and minutes are subject to standards. If there were no recognized time zones in the world how could telecommunications, or travel by land or air be regulated? And machines, the vehicles and appliances we use in our daily lives, need to be inspected from time to time— some of them every day—to ensure that they are working properly.

It is easy to foretell what the result would be if the engines, the brakes, and the various gauges and instruments in cars, trains, and aeroplanes were never checked. But people never imagine that there might be something in their own mechanism that needs to be checked. They think that they are above all that. And this is why there are so many accidents. All the difficulties and disasters that befall human beings are caused by the defects of their intellects, hearts, and wills. This is why, from time to time, they should inspect these instruments. They have been given to them to enable them to think, and love, and work, and it is absolutely essential that every day—and not just once, but three, five, ten times a day—they should regulate them with reference to the norms of the divine world.

Just as the Office of Weights and Measures at Sèvres regulates standards and norms on the physical plane, there is a cosmic office of standards which provides the criteria we need on other planes. The scriptures say that God created the universe according to divine weights and measures and numbers. The whole of creation comes from this divine office of standards, and it is to it that we must go in order to check our own instruments, our minds, and hearts, and wills.

Each period of silence during our meetings provides a golden opportunity for this work of revision, and you should take advantage of it to tune your instruments to the divine diapason, the universal soul, God himself. In this way you will be in tune once again with cosmic harmony. Until you make up your minds to work at this you will always be out of tune. What do we see musicians doing? They are constantly obliged to tune their instruments. Why is it so difficult for human beings to apply to the psychic plane things that they understand and apply without hesitation on the physical plane?

I know that some people think that it is humiliating to be obliged continually to adjust to norms. Personally, I have never found it humiliating. I have never been ashamed to say that I want my opinions to conform to the divine norm. Some people may think that if I do not cling to my own personal opinions it is because I have no dignity or independence, and they consider this a weakness. Well, they can think what they like, but that which many consider to be a mark of dignity or independence is seen by initiates as a sign of weakness, and that which others see as weakness, initiates see as true strength. The mark of true dignity is to defer to the universal office of standards. We must base ourselves on the norms of the higher world, not on those of this world below.

I am sure that many of you will object that if you all conform to the same norms you will all be exactly like each other, that each individual will just be one of a series. No, you need not worry about that. You will always be different. Your individual temperaments, abilities, and qualities are all different, and this means that you will not all work with the same methods. Look at how many different kinds of yoga the disciples of Indian masters have to choose from: Raja-yoga, the yoga of self-mastery; Karma-yoga, the yoga of self-abnegation and altruistic action; Hatha-yoga, control of one's physical body; Kriya-yoga, the work with light; Laya-yoga, the work with the Kundalini force; Bakhti-yoga, prayer, adoration, and contemplation; Jnana-yoga, meditation and knowledge; Agni-yoga, the path of love and of fire. As disciples we can all practise different forms of yoga, therefore, but the aim of each form is the same. They all teach us to raise ourselves to a higher level and draw closer to the universal principle of truth.

It is not possible to find truth if we remain within the narrow circle of our ordinary, mundane preoccupations. To find truth we have to go out of ourselves. I was still very young when I realized this, when I sensed that salvation lay in reaching beyond the limitations imposed by heredity, family, and society. It was then that I decided that I would be led by those great beings who had already explored the paths of light. And since that day I have never stopped learning. Day and night I am always learning. Yes, even at night. For sleep is simply an extension in another mode of the activities of our waking hours. If you endeavour, during the day, to rise above your prosaic, self-centred concerns and reach a higher, broader level of consciousness, sleep will give you conditions that will help you to go on with your work. Your soul leaves your body and travels through space, exploring other regions and making the acquaintance of their inhabitants. And even if, on waking, you remember none of what you have seen and heard, your travels leave profound traces within you which will gradually transform your understanding of reality.

Chapter Three

THE LINK WITH THE CENTRE

The whole of your future can be summed up in a single question: which way are you going? Are you going inwards or outwards? Towards the centre or towards the periphery?

Human existence is such that people are continually obliged to go out of themselves. As soon as they wake up in the morning they move towards the outer world. They look and listen and talk to others. They leave home and go out to work, or to shop for food or things they need for their work. They go for walks, visit friends, travel, or look for entertainment. This is all perfectly normal, but in the long run many people become so absorbed in their different external activities that they lose touch with themselves. They no longer know who they really are. And when this happens, not only do they make many mistakes because they no longer perceive things correctly, but they quickly become debilitated, and the slightest mishap or adversity cripples them. It is normal for human beings to go out of themselves. Every time we are in touch with the outer world we are obliged to leave our inner sanctum. But if we are to avoid being totally cut off from ourselves we must constantly strive to maintain the balance between the inner and the outer worlds, between the periphery and the centre.

Unfortunately, we have to recognize that human beings take pleasure in dispersion and dissipation. Their philosophical systems and the ideologies they concoct reflect this tendency to cut themselves off from the centre. More and more, everything possible is being done to lead men and women away from their source. In religion and science, and particularly in the arts, the chasm that separates them from the centre becomes ever wider until, finally, everything is scattered and disconnected and nobody understands anything any more. You will say that that is life. That the world is full of so many different people and situations that we could hardly expect it to be otherwise. Well, it is true that life is very complex. But this does not mean that the way we understand and resolve problems has to be complicated. It can be very simple. Truth is always very simple.

For the initiates everything is simple because

they have learned to reduce the infinite number of facts and situations to a few basic principles. What are these principles? They are geometrical figures. This idea may come as a surprise to you, but have you never wondered why some philosophical traditions represented God as the supreme geometer? It was because the great beings who founded these traditions understood that the multiplicity of animate and inanimate beings in the universe and the intricate relationships between them could all be reduced to the extremely simple principles represented by such geometrical figures as a circle, a triangle, a square, a pyramid or a cross.[1]

Take a circle, for instance. It is very interesting to see how we proceed when drawing a circle. We start by placing the point of the compass where we want the centre of the circle to be, and it is only by keeping this point firmly on the spot that it is possible to draw a circumference. The centre comes first therefore. A circumference can be drawn only if a centre already exists. This is why initiates see a circle as the symbol of creation, because it expresses the idea that everything that exists is linked to the centre and can only continue to exist and prosper if that link is maintained.

[1] See *The Symbolic Language of Geometrical Figures*, Izvor Collection No. 218.

Those who sever their link with the centre can no longer have a clear perception of the world or of the entities and forces at work in it. And not only that: they deprive themselves of the tide of pure life flowing from this centre, from God, the source. The equilibrium of cosmic life is founded on the uninterrupted relationship between the centre and the periphery. All the parts of the whole must converge on the centre, for it is the centre that ensures their continued existence. The perfect illustration of this is the solar system, in which the planets revolve tirelessly in harmonious orbit round the sun.

Whatever problems we may have to contend with in life, we must never forget this law of the supremacy of the centre. For centre and circumference are not only two different geometrical locations. More importantly, they represent the focal points of forces that take hold of us, and the forces of the centre, of the spirit, regenerate, whereas those of the periphery, of matter, crush and annihilate us.

Of course, the structure of human beings and the lives they lead are such that they cannot concentrate exclusively on the centre and forget about the periphery. They are obliged to turn towards the periphery, that is, to study and use matter. But that does not mean that they have to break away from the centre. On the contrary, we must all remain firmly attached to the divine centre within us, for it is the centre that unites, assembles, and explains everything, and it is perfectly possible to reach out from it to the periphery. Progressively, as you continue to renew your ties to the centre, you will be building a strong inner anchorage, and once you are firmly bound to this anchorage—or, to use a different analogy, once you have put down strong roots—you can safely venture out to the periphery.

It is well worth meditating on this question of the link with the centre, for it is absolutely essential. Life cannot exist without it. When we incarnate on this earth we begin by spending nine months in the womb, in which we are linked to our mother by the umbilical cord. After nine months this cord has to be cut so that we may live our own life as individuals. At this point we say that we are born. But in order to go on living we still have to be linked to the universe by a more tenuous, fluidic cord, and we die only when this cord is cut. Finally, there is a third, even subtler cord that links us to God. It is this cord that many people cut, and although they may say that they are alive, the truth is that they are not. They are dead. Something essential within them has died. Having severed their link with the divine source of light and warmth they drift away and lose themselves in the cold and darkness. They are spiritually dead. They may still be alive on other levels, because the cord that ties them to mother nature still exists, but on the spiritual level they are dead, and the repercussions of this spiritual death is inevitably felt in every aspect of their existence.

A disciple who is obliged to spend his days in the noise and agitation of the periphery knows very well that he needs to strengthen the ties that bind him to the centre if he is not to lose his balance and be cut adrift. The treasures to be found at the periphery are great and very alluring, that is true, but you can benefit to the full from the exploration of all those treasures only if you remain linked to the centre. Life continually places men and women in situations that threaten to unbalance them, and if they are not firmly attached to the centre they fall. And to fall means many different things. It means to live in a state of disorder and uncertainty, conflict, and illness—an endless succession of illnesses—because one has severed one's link with the one thing that is truly essential.

There is one particular area of activity in which the necessity of remaining firmly attached to the centre becomes very obvious, and that is the exploration of the subconscious. It is very dangerous to plunge into the depths of the subconscious if one has not first worked to forge a strong bond with one's divine centre within, one's higher self. The subconscious is like the abyss at the bottom of the ocean. Imagine how you would feel if you had to go down into the depths of the ocean, all alone and without lights, or protection, or experience of any kind. How terrifying to have to make your way amongst the giant seaweeds, threatened on all sides by enormous sea-monsters! Well, this is what the subconscious is, and it is very perilous to venture into it without making sure that you are firmly anchored to the divine centre of light and strength. This is why psychoanalysis, when practised by competent people with high moral standards, can produce good results, but it is still a very risky method, and its widespread use is a great danger to mankind.

As you can see, the symbolism of the circle and its centre has far-reaching implications. Seen in the abstract, all the symbols represented by geometrical figures are extremely simple. Once one begins to study the many ways in which they apply to the different levels of human activity, however, they become so diverse and complex that one can hardly recognize them any more as a circle, a triangle, a square, or a cross. But it is precisely this that interests me. The only things that really interest me are principles, general rules. Do not ask me to talk to you about details. I leave that to the specialists. They have the time to take one tiny segment of reality and explore it in minute detail. There are so many specialists that they can share out the work between them, and each one, if he feels like it, can make a name for himself as an authority in his particular field. But for my part, it is the whole that interests me. I am a complete dunce when it comes to details, so you would do better not to ask me.

The only thing that really matters is to strive to turn back to the centre. Of course, it is difficult to distinguish with any certainty whether a particular path that lies before us leads to the centre or to the periphery. It takes years and years of hard work to acquire a yardstick, a prototype that enables us to discern this. But once we have a frame of reference we are in a position to tell whether certain conditions, persons, or things will lead us closer to or further from the centre; whether a close relationship with someone, a particular business proposition, or a new enterprise will strengthen or weaken our ties with the centre.

You might say that all this is simply a question of discernment. True, but it is very difficult to explain exactly what discernment is. It is a faculty that has more to do with sensation than with understanding. We acquire it through observation, reflection, meditation, and prayer. Above all, through prudence and vigilance. It is very important to analyse oneself after every experience, so as to see whether one is moving forward or back on the path that leads to the centre. For my part, I worked for years and years to acquire this faculty, this kind of direction finder. And you can do the same. If you apply your mind to perfecting your faculty of discernment you will always take the right direction, whatever the circumstances. You must remember that I shall not always be there to answer your questions, find solutions to your problems, or give you advice. One day you are going to have to get along on your own. What will you do if you have never learned how to discern the right direction?

I have already given you methods and exercises to help you to restore your links with your own inner centre. Most of these exercises involve the sun, for, as I have said, the solar system is an ideal representation of a harmonious relationship between the centre and the periphery. But today I want to give you a new, different exercise. It is simply this: from time to time, stop whatever you are doing, close your eyes, enter in to yourself and try to get in touch with the pure fountainhead of life, your own inner centre.

To open and close your eyes is one of the things you do most often in your daily life, but you never learn anything from it because you do it unconsciously. Henceforth try to do this exercise consciously. Close your eyes slowly. Keep them closed for a few moments, and then slowly open them again, while observing the changes that take

place within you. Little by little you will begin to
understand the correspondence between the act of
opening or closing your eyes and what goes on in
your inner life. To open one's eyes is to go out
towards the periphery. To close one's eyes is to
return to the centre of one's being, God. Once you
are in touch with this centre you will sense an
influx of currents that bring you balance, peace and
harmony, and from then on, whatever you
undertake, you will know that you are moving
towards truth.

Chapter Four

REACHING FOR THE TOP

If you observe the behaviour of human beings you will notice that each individual sees people and things from his own point of view, depending on his race, nationality, religion, sex, social standing, education, profession, age, and so on... depending, above all, on his degree of evolution. This is perfectly normal. So normal, in fact, that everybody agrees that it could not be otherwise.

In reality the structure of all human beings is the same. They have all been built to the same design in the Lord's workshops. They possess the same elements and are driven by the same motive forces. Their differences stem from the fact that each one has followed a different path in descending to the material plane. And as the experience of each one has been different, from these various experiences have arisen opinions, tastes, and tendencies that are not only different but often diametrically opposed to those of others. And now, as each individual is convinced that his own view of truth represents the whole truth, it is no longer possible for them to understand each other, hence all the misunderstandings and conflicts that we see on every level.

If human beings are ever to live in harmony again, if they are ever to understand and adhere to the same values, they are going to have to take the upward path that leads to the summit, to the luminous regions of the spirit. If, instead of remaining down below, arguing and squabbling among themselves, they would only make up their minds to see things from the perspective of the summit, all their political, economic, social, and religious problems would be resolved within twenty-four hours. For there is one important truth that should be firmly fixed in your minds: if you want to solve your problems you must not remain on the level on which they arise. You must work inwardly so as to reach a higher level and look at them from above. As long as human beings are content to discuss their differences on the lowest level, not only will they never find the solutions they need, but their problems will become more and more complicated, both for the world at large and, especially, for each individual.

You at least can make this effort. You at least can make it a habit to focus on the summit, on the highest point, the point from which the truth about all beings and all things can be seen. Of course, the summit is so far away that it is totally inaccessible. Only those whose lives are perfectly pure and holy can hope to attain the topmost peak. But each one of you can strive to reach that peak by means of your thoughts, for thought is like a rope with a grappling iron on the end of it. You throw the grappling iron up as high as you can, and then you climb up the rope. This is what mountaineers do: they throw a rope and climb up on it. Yes, it seems to me that you have never seen this correspondence between the physical and the spiritual worlds.

The advantage of trying to reach the top is that on the way there you have to climb up through all the intervening regions, and in this way you get to know their inhabitants. It is more than likely that you will never actually reach the top, but what matters is to start climbing. Take the example of mountaineers again: they do not begin by trying to climb Everest. They know that that would be madness. They begin by practising on peaks of five or six thousand feet, and even the attainment of such modest heights is a cause for rejoicing. This is what counts: to get to the top of each successive stage.

When you fix your sights on reaching the top,

you are continually obliged to move forward. Each step takes you a little higher, and you begin to sense that the beneficial effects of this mental attitude are reflected in other aspects of your everyday life. When you have to put up with something very difficult, or have a problem to solve, or an important decision to make, you will find that you are less likely to be overwhelmed by the situation because you are looking at it from a higher viewpoint, from farther away. Also you will be less and less likely to act rashly or unwisely.

The peak, the summit, is not only physically higher than the rest. Every peak is a vital centre of the purest and most penetrating energies, and these energies are essential to all living creatures. A peak represents the dwelling place of omnipotence, the omnipotence of the spirit. Only the powers of the peak can command the beings of all the different realms of nature to help and protect us. We find indications of this in many accounts of the lives of saints and hermits who lived in an arid, hostile environment in which they had little food and were afflicted by fierce heat or bitter cold. A plant, an animal, or a human being always appeared to provide the food, or drink, or shelter they needed.

Several such tales are to be found in the Bible. One of them, in the Book of Kings, is about the prophet Elijah:

And the word of the Lord came unto him, saying, Get thee hence, and turn thee eastward, and hide thyself by the brook Cherith, that is before Jordan. And it shall be that thou shalt drink of the brook; and I have commanded the ravens to feed thee there. So he went and did according unto the word of the Lord... And the ravens brought him bread and flesh in the morning, and bread and flesh in the evening; and he drank of the brook. And it came to pass after a while that the brook dried up, because there had been no rain in the land. And the word of the Lord came unto him, saying, Arise, get thee to Zarephath, which belongeth to Zidon, and dwell there: behold, I have commanded a widow woman there to sustain thee. So he arose and went to Zarephath. And when he came to the gate of the city, behold, the widow woman was there gathering of sticks...

When the orders come from on high, from the topmost peak, both nature and human beings are bound to obey.

There is nothing intrinsically wrong in devoting a great deal of attention to the things of the physical, astral, or mental planes. If they are pure and luminous the results you obtain may be considerable, but they will never equal those that come from striving to reach the peak, the quintessence that orders and controls the whole of

creation. When you reach the summit you reach the
nodal point of the forces on which all else depends.

Have you understood what I am trying to say?
No, I am not sure that you really grasp my
meaning. Let me take an example from medicine.
When someone is suffering from severe anaemia
none of his organs functions properly. What should
he do? Try to care for his brain, his stomach, his
liver, lungs, and intestines one after the other? No,
that would be an endless task. He only needs a
blood transfusion, and all his organs will be
restored to health. In the same way, when you
touch your inner summit, you receive a transfusion
of pure, vivifying energies, because it is there, at
the summit, that the omnipotence of the spirit is at
work.

I have already explained how initiates use
geometrical figures as symbols to explain the major
questions of philosophy and life. We have already
talked about the circle, but now let us look at the
symbolism of a cross. A cross consists of two lines,
vertical and horizontal. The horizontal line
symbolizes dispersion, the movement of water
spreading over the ground. The vertical line
symbolizes unification, the movement of fire
leaping heavenwards. The horizontal line therefore
signifies matter, and the vertical signifies the spirit.
And, as you see, these two lines are not separate
and apart, they are joined to each other, and this

shows that they are not incompatible. The symbol of the cross bids us accomplish our work on the material plane while at the same time espousing the upward movement of the vertical line and striving to reach the spirit, the fountainhead, the summit.

Chapter Five

FROM MULTIPLICITY TO UNITY

I

Truth must necessarily embrace the totality, all beings, both animate and inanimate. Truth is one. In oneness everything is included, everything is understood, all questions are resolved. Those who pierce the secret of the number One—or of the letter Aleph א—understand all the other numbers, all the other letters. In other words, they understand all the powers of the universe. For the Logos— numbers and letters—is one seamless substance. In the Logos there is no separation, no division: all the elements are joined to each other; each element is an integral component of one supreme entity. This is why anyone who wants to make real progress on the path of initiation must concentrate on oneness.

What is the One? On paper it is a simple, unadorned vertical line: 1. At first sight there is nothing very significant about it, and yet it is the dynamic creative principle, the source of life.

When I was still a young disciple in Bulgaria the Master Peter Deunov often invited me to go and talk to him. One day he took a book of numerology in English from the bookcase and began to translate for me the first chapter, which dealt with the number One. Naturally, I was interested and listened attentively as he read, but I must admit that I was not particularly concerned about the One at that time. It seemed to me that the other numbers were more important, that they contained greater, richer secrets. When he came to the end of the first chapter I expected him to go on to the chapters that dealt with the other numbers, but I was wrong. He closed the book, put it back on the shelf, and that was the end of my visit.

I was burning with eagerness to learn more. On my way home I thought, 'Surely the next time the Master invites me to go and talk to him he will go on with the book.' But this was not to be. He never referred to it again. For a time I kept expecting him to read some more and was rather disappointed when he did not, but as I had tremendous faith in my Master I knew that there was always a reason for what he did. Finally, I told myself that the fact that he said nothing about the other numbers meant that they were not very important. I did not need to learn about them. After thinking and meditating on

the One, I understood that all the other numbers
were contained in and flowed from the One. At first
sight the Master had given me very little, but in fact
he had opened a door on to the infinite for me.

The One is sacred because it represents the
whole. The entire cosmos is a single, unbroken
unity. We may see what seems like separateness,
ruptures and boundaries, but in reality there is no
absolute division anywhere. The refraction of light
through a prism is the most striking illustration of
this. Here is a beam of white light, which
represents the One, and when it is passed through a
prism it is broken up into seven colours. Is it not
extraordinary to see how this single white ray of
light produces the diversity of the seven colours—
violet, indigo, blue, green, yellow, orange, and red?
Is there anything that can demonstrate more
strikingly than light the passage from unity to
diversity, and from diversity to unity? If you look at
those colours and try to determine where red ends
and orange begins, for instance, if you try to
discern a boundary, a line of separation between
them, you will fail. You cannot see it because it
does not exist. There is no separation. This example
of light is particularly interesting because light is
the very substance of the universe.

In reality, therefore, there are no boundaries or
limits. All is One. This is true even of a human
being. The ideal human being represents the One.

Let me give you another very simple example taken from an area that everyone is familiar with, that of health. When you are well nothing more needs to be said. People ask how you are, and you reply, 'Fine!' One word says it all. But if you are ill… Oh, what a song and dance! From your head to your toes there are so many parts of the body that can hurt, and so many different ways that they can fail to function properly. And you know how difficult it is, when you are ill, to eat, drink, sleep, breathe, walk, hear, see, work, or study. Health, you see, is one. There are not two or three different healths. Illness, on the other hand, is multiple. There are an infinite number of different illnesses. We do not even know them all, for new ones are constantly appearing, brought on by the unreasonable way people live.

The function of our organs is to work together to maintain the oneness of health, life. For health is one; life is one. Illness and death, on the other hand, are separation, division, dislocation. All our efforts should lead us towards the oneness that is synonymous with simplicity. Salvation lies in the simplicity of the One. Unfortunately, simplicity does not appeal to human beings. It bores them. They find it dull, and think that the spice of diversity is far more interesting. Is there any wonder that they are ill?

I have already told you that the initiates

synthesize even the most complex problems by
presenting them in the form of geometrical figures.
Take a pyramid, for example. I have visited the great
pyramids of Cheops, Chephren, and Mykerinos,
and meditated on the science that the ancient
Egyptian initiates sought to synthesize in these
extraordinary monuments. A pyramid consists of
four triangular planes erected on a large square
base and joined at the top. The base of a pyramid
symbolizes the multiplicity of phenomena, and its
summit the world of principles, unity. On the lower
level, the level of phenomena, we are dispersed and
in a state of confusion, because we cannot quite
place people or things, or see how they relate to
each other. If we want a clear view we need to be
on a higher level. And what does this mean? It
means that we have to take the path of unity. It is
unity, oneness, that governs, coordinates, and
guides multiplicity. On the level of unity we are at
the heart of reality and can see the warp and woof
of the fabric of life.

The things of the physical plane are always
seen as disparate, unrelated facts or events, and for
this reason it is impossible to sort out one's
problems if one tries to deal with them only on that
level. And this brings us back to what I was saying
about working with an image of the summit. Let
me repeat it here: you will never resolve your
problems if you try to do so on the level on which

they arise. You can only do so by rising higher, always higher, until you can look at them from the vantage point of unity.

II

You must make up your minds to study the science of unity in greater depth, for it is this science that will show you how the different elements of creation are linked. Unfortunately, human beings tend to neglect the question of unity. One hears it discussed from time to time, of course, but where and when? Not always for the best reasons. More often than not people feel the need of unity only when they want others to join forces with them in order to defeat an opponent or a political party, or to wage war against another country. When it comes to resisting those whom they see as enemies, they are ready to call for unity. But this, of course, is not true unity. True unity never combats or excludes anyone. On the contrary.

If you work at raising your mind to the summit that represents unity you will begin to get the feeling that all human beings are linked. And this is quite true. On a higher level we form a unit. Each one of us is a cell of the great cosmic body, and each single cell reflects the entire body. Those who injure others in the belief that they are separate entities, and that they are not thereby injuring themselves, are deluding themselves. When we harm someone else we are always harming ourselves, even though we may not feel it at the time.

Some might say that if they really worked to attain the unity I am talking about they would end up by being exactly like everybody else. No, that is not so. Try to understand: I am not saying that all human beings should think the same thoughts or have the same desires, the same tastes, and the same activities. Life offers a tremendous diversity of possibilities. It is only in essentials that we must be one.

Take some very simple examples from everyday life, such as nutrition and breathing. All human beings need food and fresh air. Whether they choose to eat wheat, maize, soya beans, or rice; or apples, oranges, bananas, or mangoes is quite beside the point. Neither does it matter where the air they breathe comes from—the mountain tops, the sea, the forest, or their own garden. The only thing that is essential is that in order to keep fit they need to eat healthy food and breathe clean air.

All this is perfectly obvious. Yes, but the truth is that a great many people in the world are deprived of these essentials. And how many of those who do enjoy good conditions ever bother their heads about the deplorable conditions in which others live? As you can see, even though everyone recognizes the basic needs of human beings, the problems are far from being resolved. And this is even more true in other areas. And to think that many people wonder why there is so much conflict in the world… What hypocrisy! Is it surprising that people rise up against a world in which they have no freedom, not enough food to feed their families, and no chance of sending their children to school? And yet, in spite of this situation, everybody is convinced that they think and live according to truth.

Only when they succeed in living together in peace and prosperity will human beings be justified in saying that they have found truth. Truth is the expression of a situation in which it is possible for all to live together in harmony, and a great many things still need to be changed, adjusted, and corrected before this is achieved. And this is our work. This is the task that has been allotted to us. But we have to realize that truth is necessarily unique and universal; that it can be found only in unity.

This is what I am talking about when I speak of unity. You must try to feel that all human beings have the same fundamental needs. Do not delude yourself: as long as you do not feel in your own flesh the privations suffered by others, and sense that the harm done to them is also done to you, you have not found truth. Of course, you do not feel this today because it does not affect you directly, but if you develop a deep awareness of unity you will feel it.

This is the unity I am talking about, therefore. It is not uniformity, and it has nothing to do with making everyone on earth fit exactly the same mould. In any case, there is no need to worry about that. Every individual is different, and there is no way to make them all alike. Many rulers and political regimes have attempted to do so, and sometimes it has almost seemed as though they had succeeded, but their apparent success never lasted very long; they were soon obliged to recognize that all such attempts were doomed from the start. There is something intractable in human beings that makes them resist all attempts at uniformity. So do not be concerned about it. Be concerned rather to gain a true understanding of what unity means on the very highest level.

Human beings are made up of three fundamental principles: mind, heart and will. The mind needs light (knowledge); the heart needs warmth (love); and the will needs to act, that is, to manifest in action the light of the mind and the warmth of the heart. It is in this sense that human beings are identical. They are identical in that their basic structure is the same, and their needs and aspirations correspond to that structure. Whether they are aware of this or not, whether they accept the idea or not, this is the truth of their being, and it is in this sense that they must work collectively.

Every day we have to strive for unity. The surest way for mankind to achieve unity is for each individual to achieve it within himself. And it is here that the greatest difficulty lies. Many people have admirable aspirations in their hearts and souls, but at the same time they are driven by other forces, by their desires and passions, to acts that lead later to shame and regret. Their inner conflicts tear them apart and eventually destroy them. Human beings need to be at peace with themselves. They need inner unity. They need their mind, heart, and will to work hand in hand. If they are continually torn by inner conflict they cannot find their equilibrium and this is the cause of much misery. Sometimes, indeed, the lack of equilibrium is so great that it leads to neurosis, and even insanity.

The true unity for which we must all strive is like that of the solar system. The sun occupies the central position, and each planet moves in orbit around it, never deviating from the route that cosmic intelligence has ordained for it. The inner unity that must be the goal of every human being is on the same pattern, and it presupposes a veritable apprenticeship, for we need to learn how to live, think, and feel in such a way that the movement of every particle of our physical and psychic being is ruled by the sun within us, our divine self, our spirit. True knowledge and power flow from this order.

The teaching of the Universal White Brotherhood has no other goal than to enable us to achieve this inner unity, the unity of the three principles of heart, mind, and will, the unity of all our physical and psychic activities, the unity of our lower and higher natures. And this unity can be achieved only if one universal principle reigns at the centre of our being and maintains the proper hierarchical order among all the different factors and binds them into one. It is thanks to this philosophy of unity that we can explain and resolve all our difficulties.

In the absence of unity there can be no truth. On the surface of it, faced with the pitiful sight of the bitter conflicts, rivalries, and wars that afflict the world, one might be tempted to think that a philosophy of duality would be closer to the truth. But in spite of their conflicts, human beings are one. To sever the bonds that bind them spells death for all, and it is precisely this that they have never understood. In spite of the conflicts that seem to disunite them, they are, in fact, nourished by unity. On the cosmic tree of unity there are innumerable branches, leaves, and fruits, and they are continually rubbing up against each other, but this cannot alter the fact that they all stem from the same trunk and the same roots, and that they are dependent on them for their very existence.

The one thing that is most important for the conduct of our life is to know that we are all one. If some of the things we see seem to contradict this, if the world sometimes seems badly designed, that is only our own opinion. We call these things evil, and we would like to do away with them, but cosmic intelligence, which knows how to use them, sees that they are good, for each is in its proper place. Cosmic intelligence is like a chemist. Chemists keep all kinds of poisons, microbes, and explosives in their laboratories, but they do not use them to poison or destroy human beings. They use them to manufacture beneficial, therapeutic substances. And if chemists are capable of doing this, can you imagine that the Lord is not equally capable? He too needs all these materials and elements that we class as evil. They serve a useful purpose in the cosmic economy. The only thing is that you have to know how to use them. The Lord, of course, knows, and we, who do not know, have to learn.

The earth too is a chemist. It never stops

producing grass, flowers, trees, vegetables, and fruit from the sewage, decaying vegetation, and dead bodies that are thrown into it. Yes, billions and billions of corpses have been buried under the soil, and the earth rejects none of them. It is a veritable cemetery, and it is this cemetery that nourishes the whole of mankind. How is this possible? It is simply that the earth possesses the secret of transformation, which is the secret of unity. You must never forget this: the secret of true transformation is the secret of unity. Why do human beings not possess this secret? To obtain it they are going to have to learn from the earth, otherwise they will end by being poisoned. This is the fate of all those who have never learned the art of transformation: they are poisoned.

Understand what I am saying: if you cannot accept the philosophy of unity you will always be ill, tormented, and inwardly divided. It is the philosophy of unity that will enable you to face up to your difficulties and give you the powers and the keys you need.

You need never fear that the quest for unity will lead to uniformity. The goal is one, but the paths that lead to it are many. For my part, I have chosen the path of Peter Deunov, which is the path of Christ. If you ask whether there are not other paths, I can assure you that indeed there are. To deny it would be untruthful. For my part, I have chosen the path that best suits me, and I intend to stick to it. I shall never deviate from it. In some ways you might consider me fanatical. But deep down I know very well that there are all kinds of other paths that lead to God. One has to be very open, very broad-minded. Each one has to choose their own path, but that does not mean that it is the only one. There is more than one way to become a true son or daughter of God. Yes, it is very important to be broadminded. There is room for all, and we all have to find our own place. There is nothing to be gained by being intolerant, narrow-minded or restrictive.

Chapter Six

BUILDING THE EDIFICE

The musicians in an orchestra—flautists, clarinetists, violinists, cellists, oboists, and so on— all have their own particular score in front of them as they play. They are not obliged to know the scores of the other players. But up in front, in full view of each member of the orchestra, is the conductor who knows the whole symphony and each individual score, and whose job is to see that each instrument comes in on time and plays with just the right volume and the right shade of feeling. However beautiful the part played by the individual musicians, if they do not respect the conductor's instructions, instead of a symphony we would hear a horrible cacophony.

And now let us see how this applies to the situation in the world today. We see a great many capable professionals—people who, you might say, know their own particular score perfectly, but who have no grasp of the symphony as a whole. That they should be proficient in their own speciality is in itself excellent, but their ignorance of the whole gives rise to all kinds of anomalies and disorders. To the extent to which they confine themselves to the ideas and attitudes engendered by their personal situation, they are incapable of a view of the whole. In other words, they are not in possession of the truth. We might think that, up to a point, this shortcoming is excusable, but in fact it is not. They should be working to become orchestra leaders or conductors themselves. In other words, they should be making every effort to rise to where they can have an accurate view of the whole, so as to be able to act correctly in all circumstances.

You will object that the point of view I am talking about is that of God, the Creator. Yes, that is true, but the task of a human being is to become more and more like God. Did Jesus not say, 'Be ye therefore perfect, even as your Father who is in heaven is perfect?' A true disciple of Jesus understands that it is essential to acquire this overall point of view, to try and see things from the viewpoint of the Creator.

Those who have a familial, social, professional, or political responsibility should constantly strive to reach that high point within themselves, from which they can have an overall view of every aspect of the problems they have to cope with. In this way, the decisions they make will be fair and well-balanced. You will say that even if their decisions are fair there is no guarantee that they will be respected, because most people are only concerned about their own selfish interests. It is not an easy matter to get them to recognize the interests of others. That is true, you may analyse certain situations with perfect accuracy and draw the right conclusions, and then find that nobody accepts them. But even if this happens it is no reason to abandon your efforts. As long as you manage to rise to this higher viewpoint there will be other occasions in life when it will prevail. When you strive to make progress on the path of lucidity and altruism no effort is ever wasted. Even if other people treat you as an impractical dreamer, a visionary, or even a lunatic—there will be no lack of epithets—it should not discourage you as long as you yourself know that you are moving towards truth.

Genuine initiates and spiritual masters are conductors. Perhaps you think that they are alone, that there is no orchestra in front of them? But that is only because you cannot see their orchestra, for it is within them. It is the cells and organs of their body that form an orchestra, and the conductor is always up there on the podium, conducting this orchestra as it sings and plays according to the score put before it. The brain, the stomach, the heart, the hands and feet, the toes, eyes, and mouth... every part of the body has its own particular function through which it contributes to the harmony of the whole body. Yes, but physical harmony is not enough, and for this reason an initiate questions his members and organs every day. To his legs he says, 'Where are you taking me?' To his arms, 'What are you about to do?' He asks his mouth what it is saying, his eyes what they are looking at, and his brain what it is thinking about. And in this way he creates and maintains harmony among them.

And now it is up to you: if you want to be conscious and intelligent disciples you are going to have to become conductors of your own orchestra. Every day you must not only make sure that your physical organs work harmoniously together to keep you healthy, but you must also guide their activity towards a higher goal, so as to avoid causing disharmony in the cosmic organism.

Whatever the subject of my talks, you will find that I constantly come back to this idea: how to make use of all the elements that exist in and around us in order to progress toward universal harmony.

Now let me take another analogy, that of a building site, where all the materials are piled up helter-skelter. If you want to know how they are all supposed to relate to each other you will have to look at the plans of the building. In other words, you will have to go up to the office of the person who designed the building, the supreme Architect, God.

Creation exists. The edifice already exists. The question that faces human beings is how to use the elements that have been put at their disposal in order to build their own edifice. For human beings are part of the great cosmic edifice, but they are also conscious, thinking beings, and this means that they have a part to play in the whole that is different from that of rocks, plants or animals. Neither is it enough for them to make an inventory of what exists; they must acquire firsthand knowledge of the different materials, and learn to use them to build their own individual lives, while at the same time helping to build the life of the collectivity.

Sooner or later, each one of us will be obliged to take an active part in the construction of this edifice of collective, universal life. All our activities must be made to converge in this direction. As long as human beings live selfish, individualistic lives, cut off from the whole, it is as though they were content to pile up materials but were incapable of organizing them and building something with them. Unfortunately, this is very often the case. Most human beings do nothing but accumulate masses of materials until they are staggering under their weight. It is high time now that they decided to build something with them. But before they can build anything useful they need to study the plans drawn up by the supreme Architect, God. In the process of becoming familiar with the Creator's designs they will be obliged to identify with him, and in this way, little by little, they will regain that part of their inner being that resembles God.

It should be no surprise to you any longer to see that whatever my starting point I always end up in the same place. Over and over again I have to remind you of the goal you should be aiming for, the construction of the edifice. As long as you are content to accumulate all kinds of miscellaneous items of knowledge and information, you may pride yourself on being 'a walking encyclopedia', but it is not this that will enable you to evolve and to contribute to the evolution of humanity as a whole. With the teaching of the initiates, on the other hand—even if your store of knowledge is very limited—you will go a long way. As long as you continually bear in mind that this edifice must be built both inwardly and in the collectivity, this idea will be your salvation. It will vivify, illuminate, and resuscitate you.

Of course, if you are capable of working unremittingly towards the construction of the edifice while at the same time becoming a mine of information, do so by all means. But although your fellow humans may consider you to be a leading light, if your erudition makes you lose sight of your mission, heaven will see only that you have burdened your soul and spirit with a lot of useless bric-a-brac.

Whatever you do and whatever you see around you, you should always try to see where things fit within the harmony of universal life. Ever since I began talking to you this is what I have always tried to do. I may be talking about some tiny detail of everyday life, but I always reach the same conclusion. Perhaps you feel like complaining, 'It's so boring… always the same thing!' Well, boring or not, this is the only thing that matters. Your constant need for variety and change is a snare. Reality is made up of an infinite number of details, and I know that the temptation to pursue each one is very strong. But all these details exist for only one reason: to contribute to a single edifice. They must all fit into the one great cosmic design. When Jesus said, 'Be ye therefore perfect, even as your Father who is in heaven is perfect,' he was saying exactly this, for to be perfect is to restore order to all our scattered elements.

Of course, there is a great deal more to the notion of perfection. It is said, for instance, that animals are perfect. Yes, on their own level, as animals, they are perfect. When they are only a few days old they are capable of walking, swimming, galloping, and they reach maturity very rapidly, whereas humans take years to be fully grown. At least, as far as their physical maturity is concerned, it takes years, but their psychic and spiritual maturity never comes to an end.

Take another example: when children begin to attend school they need to be 'perfect'. That is, they need arms and legs, eyes, ears, and a brain that function correctly. If they are physically or mentally handicapped everything becomes much more difficult. They will not get ahead if their physical and psychic organs are not in good working order. Similarly, when initiatic science teaches that human beings must be perfect, it means first and foremost that their psychic and spiritual organs must be well developed and in good working order. Only if this is the case can human beings strive for the perfection of God, who is the fullness of knowledge, love, and power.

A certain number of you have reached this first degree of 'perfection', the stage at which it becomes possible—as long as you continue to work at it, both in this life and in each successive incarnation—eventually to attain the perfection of God himself. Only when you achieve this will it be true to say that you have contributed to the construction of the edifice. So there you are, one has to be perfect in order to become perfect... Is it clear? Do you understand what I am saying?

Chapter Seven

CONTEMPLATING TRUTH:
ISIS UNVEILED

I

Do you know what my dearest wish is? It is to be useful to you. Yes, this is my constant preoccupation: to give you something today that I have not already given you, a new element, a new truth. 'Is that possible?' you might ask, 'How can a truth be new?' Yes, it is perfectly possible, for the eternal principle of truth towards which we must all strive is made up of a multitude of truths, just as a living organism is made up of millions and millions of cells. And no words, no book can reveal to us the whole of this eternal truth in which all truths are contained. The only way we can approach the perfect, sublime quintessence of absolute truth is by a gradual, progressive grasp of lesser truths.

For years and years I have done nothing but lay before you the multiple aspects of truth as they appear in the physical, astral, mental, causal, buddhic, and atmic worlds, in the hope that one day you may reach the one great truth that embraces all that exists.

When we see the beauty and the profound insight that reveals itself in certain works of art—poems, paintings, or music—or in certain philosophical, initiatic, or mystical writings, we realize that their authors must have contemplated a truth that is not visible to others. We can perceive this kind of truth only if we have eyes other than those of our physical body. The powers of our physical organs of sight are very limited. They cannot see very much of what the initiates call reality unless they themselves are illuminated by a light that enables them to see beyond physical appearances. What kind of eyes are capable of seeing beyond appearances? And what is the light that illuminates the world they see?

Truth is a real world, a world of light, beauty, harmony, and perfection, and in order to penetrate this world something within us must be attuned to the same wavelength. We all possess a higher faculty that is capable of seeing truth, but as that faculty has never been unlocked and set in motion, we still have some work to do to make it operational. This is the faculty that we call intuition. It is a faculty of the spirit.

Truth will forever elude the grasp of human beings if they continue to conceive it as knowledge of the physical world, the world that they can see, weigh, and measure. The physical world is no more than a manifestation, a remote consequence of truth. We see it and think that we are seeing truth, but what we see is only a garment, the outer husk of truth. Truth is a world of perfection, and it manifests itself on three planes: spiritual, psychic, and physical. On the spiritual plane it manifests itself through the virtues; on the psychic plane it manifests itself through our thoughts and feelings; and on the physical plane it manifests itself through forms, colours, sound, and so on.

It is a fallacy to think that the intellect can know truth. The intellect is a faculty that enables us to know the physical world and a little of the psychic world, but no more. Of itself, the intellect cannot know truth; its scope is too narrow. Take a very simple example, that of a rose. To know the whole truth of a rose is not simply a question of perceiving its form, colour, and scent. The truth of a rose is an emanation, a presence that is beyond the grasp of the intellect. To know a rose is to sense all the different elements that make it a rose and nothing else. And this applies with even greater truth to a human being. The truth of a human being is the summary and synthesis of all his constituent elements, from his spirit to his physical body. As long as you do not know all these elements you do not know the whole truth about him, only a very small part. The truth of a human being, the complete and absolute truth, is in the spirit, and can be known only by the spirit.

You will perhaps say, 'All right, I admit that it is very difficult to know a human being. But nature is something else. We do know nature.' No, even nature is unknown to you. You do not know what a rose is, and you do not know what the earth is. All that you see around you—forests, mountains, rivers, and oceans—all this is no more than the outer wrappings of nature, the layers of physical matter that clothe the earth. You have to go beyond this outer aspect and learn to see and sense the vibrations and emanations of the etheric body of nature. In fact, the etheric body, too, is a cloak; we have to see even beyond this.

Only those who are capable of divesting nature of its outer garments can know truth. This was the whole purpose of the ancient initiations: to teach the disciples to draw aside the veil of Isis. In the religion of ancient Egypt the goddess Isis was the spouse of the god Osiris. She was the great feminine figure in whom the initiates saw a symbol of primordial nature, the matrix from which came all beings and all the elements of creation. It is this mysterious nature, impenetrable by ordinary men and women, that is the principal object of study of the initiates. In order to penetrate its secrets they endeavour to understand all the forms of existence to which it has given rise and through which it manifests itself.

To speak of 'Isis unveiled' is to evoke an image. An image that may be completely misunderstood by some—they immediately imagine a lewd scene in which they strip a woman of her clothes. But this has nothing to do with the reality. The initiates never touch a woman, for they know that what they are seeking is elsewhere. Their ambition is to lift the veil of nature, and they can do so only through the greatest possible purity and absolute self-mastery. Only in these conditions will Isis consent to reveal herself to them in all her glory.

For an initiate true knowledge is a lifting of the veil. What a pity that the understanding of nudity should be so obscured by all the prejudices and taboos that have grown up over the centuries, which always associate it with sexuality. There are people who can never hear or read the word nudity without their imagination immediately running away with them. It is time now to look beyond the physical aspect and see that the notion of nudity can be transposed on to higher planes. Actually, even on the purely physical plane it can be understood differently. Instead of envisaging only the external, concrete fact of nudity you have to learn to interpret it. For example, the instinct that urges men to undress a woman is an expression of a human being's deep-seated need to strip away the outer wrappings that are an obstacle to knowledge. Of course, if a man does nothing more than undress a woman's physical body, that will not help him to know her any better. Even without clothes her true self will still be hidden, mysterious, impenetrable, for the physical body is also a cloak. Even our subtler bodies are cloaks.

When clairvoyants practise dissociation in order to work and learn on the astral plane, they shrug off their physical bodies as though they were shrugging off a garment, and then their astral bodies can travel freely through space. But like the physical body, the astral body, too, is an encumbrance, a garment that prevents us from seeing reality. Even the mental body has to be cast aside. Only then can we be utterly naked and free, with no barrier between ourselves and truth. To think that there is any other way to know truth is the equivalent of thinking that you could know someone simply because you had passed them in the street. No, in order to know someone you have to go beyond not only the barriers of their clothes but also those of their different bodies, until you reach the spirit. When we enter the region of the spirit we are entering a region of forces without form, an ocean of life and joy, in which we are free to breathe and to expand without limits.

Only the spirit is naked and needs no clothes. It puts on clothes when it wants to manifest itself on the material plane, but when it is 'at home' it undresses. If human beings knew how to interpret their everyday gestures they would realize that they constantly mirror this alternation between the descent into the realm of matter and the upward movement to the realm of the spirit. When you dress in the morning you start with your underclothes and light garments, such as shirts and blouses, and end with a jacket or overcoat. In the same way, when we incarnate we put on our heavier, denser bodies over the lighter ones. And when we undress before going to bed, we reverse the process and take off our different layers of clothing. And all this is symbolic, for we are going to have to do the same thing when we leave this world. We have to dress in order to descend, and undress in order to rise. To take off one's clothes is, symbolically, to go beyond the opaque world of appearances and discover reality.

The veil that conceals Isis is the mystery of living nature that we have not yet pierced. And when I speak of nature, I include human nature, for human nature, too, is hidden by veils. This is why it is so difficult for human beings to know themselves and each other. True knowledge requires that we rise to the sublime regions of the spirit. Only when we cease to see ourselves and others through the distorting lens of our opaque bodies shall we be able to see the true immensity, light, and splendour of human beings on the higher, sublime planes.

All the hierophants of the past taught their disciples the same truth: a human being is a reflection of nature. Both are veiled. Beneath the layers of matter dwells a spirit, a spark, an indescribable, omniscient, all-powerful being, God himself. To those who, through discipline, prayer, and self-denial, are capable of fulfilling the demands of the spirit, Isis will reveal herself without her veils.

II

What does it mean to say that someone is naked? One of two things: either that he is poor, destitute, bereft of all qualities and virtues; or that he is concealed by no external shell or wrappings, that he is free, perfect, true. Only divine beings are naked in this second sense, and this quality is sometimes expressed by saying that they are robed in light. It is very difficult to find words to express adequately the realities of the spiritual life. We have to resort to analogies, comparisons, and symbols. This is why initiates say that in the divine world truth is naked, meaning that it is not hidden under layers of camouflage. They might equally say that truth is pure light, for light is a reality that lies on the borderline between the material and the spiritual worlds.

Nature offers certain indications of these correspondences between the physical and the spiritual planes. In summer, for instance, when the sun shines and gives great light and heat, we wear fewer clothes. In winter, when there is less sunshine and consequently less light and heat, we wear more. Heat and cold are symbols of the inner life. The greater the distance between ourselves and the divine world, the colder we are and the poorer in virtue. This is why we are obliged to wrap ourselves in layers of rags, because we are far from the source of heat and light. Whereas when we live a pure and luminous life that brings us closer to the source, we can discard all these useless layers. You must learn to interpret all these symbols of the psychic life.

You must understand that the nudity I am talking about is the nudity of the astral and mental bodies. Because of your selfish, malicious, spiteful thoughts and feelings you have made these bodies so opaque that you are no longer capable of making contact with the realities of the spiritual world and its inhabitants. You would like to meditate perhaps, but as you have never managed to free yourself from your prosaic interests and concerns, from your feelings of envy, irritation, and resentment, or from burdensome memories of the past, you are incapable of rising to a higher plane. However long you sit there with your eyes closed, waiting for the mechanism to be set in motion and your soul to soar to realms of light, nothing happens. In such a situation it is almost pointless even to try to meditate. You will get nowhere. Your inner instruments cannot function; they are too clogged with dirt. And this will always be the case until you learn to discard all your old, heavy, dirty, ragged clothes. Yes, symbolically speaking, you are wearing a great many old clothes that need to be discarded.

The most important thing in life, therefore, is to work to divest yourself of all these heavy, opaque layers. This is a very difficult task, I know. In fact, not only is it difficult to do, but many people find it difficult even to understand that these clothes actually exist, or why they should get rid of them.

Truth alone is naked. To be capable of rising to the level of truth we must work to free ourselves inwardly from all that is opaque, all that screens us from the divine world. Once we attain a state of nakedness it is possible to rise to great heights and receive messages, advice, wisdom, love, and help from God. We have to be stripped naked in order to enter heaven. That is, we have to have divested ourselves of all covetousness, self-interest, and false conceptions. The freer we are from all encumbrances, the higher we can rise.

After our meditation, when we come down— for as long as we are on earth we always have to come down again and get on with our work on earth—we put on our clothes. That is, we go back to our normal work, to our normal activities with our families and friends, neighbours, business colleagues, and so on. For the world we have to be clothed, but not for heaven. Heaven welcomes us only if we are undressed.

So this is the magnificent image that the initiates gave us when they spoke of contemplating the naked truth, Isis unveiled. I shall say no more about it today. It is up to you now to meditate so as to understand what the veil of Isis means and how to strip it away in order to know truth.

Chapter Eight

GARMENT OF LIGHT

A garment is something material that envelops and hides us; it is also a protection from the outside world. If you wear a thick coat you will be protected not only from the cold, but also from insect bites or from accidental blows, whereas if you are naked you will be vulnerable to the slightest aggression. The more layers of clothing you take off, the more vulnerable or sensitive you will be. And if we apply this law to our inner life we see that sensitivity is a manifestation of spirituality, and that we have to strip away the layers of our ordinary concerns in order to become more sensitive to the divine world.

The Bible has stories about people who, having lived in conformity with divine law, having overcome temptation and conquered evil, received a garment as a reward. Sometimes the garment was white, sometimes coloured, but it was always described as a magnificent robe of precious cloth. As I have already explained, this robe symbolizes the aura.[1] The aura is our true garment. To earn it we have to shed all that makes us heavy and dark so as to be capable of being in contact with the divine world. The aura, this robe of light, is a sign that we have succeeded.

You will say that I started by talking about nudity, and now I am talking about clothes. Yes, because to speak of nudity is only one way of expressing things. As I have said, there are so few words with which to express the spiritual life that we have to use analogies that may sometimes seem to contradict each other. In reality, a human being is never entirely naked, for we are clothed not only in the physical body, but also in our subtler bodies. The inner work we would have to accomplish in order to be completely naked is so immense as to be almost impossible. It consists in becoming pure spirit, or to put it more accurately, in investing the indwelling spirit with such power that it is as though the physical body were pulverized and transformed into light. This is what the disciples witnessed when Jesus was transfigured before them.

---

[1] See *Man's Subtle Bodies and Centres*, Izvor Collection, No. 219, Chapter 2.

This question of a garment is very interesting. It is worth taking the time to talk about it. The physical body is the garment of the soul and spirit. Words are the garments of thought. Feelings, thoughts, and forces all have garments. All creatures visible and invisible are clothed. A flower, for example, is a garment that conceals a living entity. This is why we should meditate on flowers, on their shape, colour, and scent, so as to learn about the nature of the beings who wear such garments. And not only on flowers, but on all that exists in the different kingdoms of nature: mineral, vegetable, animal, and human. Crystals, diamonds, precious stones... these are all garments in which spiritual entities manifest themselves on the physical plane.

It takes a great deal of knowledge to understand this question of garments, that is, to interpret the forms taken by all creatures, all entities. A garment is a condensation of subtle elements, and it is extremely difficult to decipher such a complexity of expressions and shades of meaning. Mountains, lakes, rivers, and trees... all these constitute the garments of the cosmic spirit. All things visible, from minerals to human beings, are garments, and these garments are of untold diversity. In the animal kingdom alone, for instance, look at the immense variety of birds and their plumage.

As I have said, clothes serve to conceal the beings that wear them, but they also provide a clue as to the nature of those beings. Why do actors wear costumes, for example? They could very well act without them, but the costumes reveal their role. As soon as an actor comes on stage, before he even opens his mouth, the audience has some idea of the kind of character he is portraying.

Shapes and colours are not the only things that constitute a garment. Movements, sounds, even scents are garments. All means of expression can be classed as garments. And this is particularly true in respect to human beings. Perhaps you are wondering whether the spirit can express itself without the concealment of a garment. No, for how could we know anything about a force, an energy, if it did not manifest itself by means of an outer form?

In order to express itself the spirit is obliged to use intermediaries, which can be of all kinds, ranging from the most densely material to the most subtle. Certain impulses express themselves through movement; others, which are subtler, express themselves by means of a look, a tone of voice, the colour or complexion of a face. A whole variety of expressions exists, therefore, from the most densely material to those that are so ethereal as to be extremely difficult to perceive and even more difficult to interpret. As you see, this question of garments is so vast and profound that one could spend a lifetime exploring it.

Chapter Nine

THE SKIN

I once received a really extraordinary letter, in which, among other things, the writer said, 'It is as though you had learned all that you know through your skin. As though it were your skin that enabled you to know things...' This remark really took me by surprise, it was so unexpected. As a matter of fact, if you think about it you will see that it is true: it is principally through the skin that a human being receives knowledge. Nothing in the way of sensations, impressions, or influences can enter a man or woman without the permission of the skin, for it is the skin that surrounds the body and its organs. Our skin is the inspector that examines and tests everything that attempts to enter us, and lets in only what we need. Each organ is the result of a gradual differentiation of the skin. In this sense the skin is like a mother who gives birth to numerous children, or like the roots of a tree, thanks to which the trunk can grow and mature and produce branches, leaves, flowers, and fruit.

Since the skin is the keeper of the gates, the one that allows or denies entrance or exit, it is important to make sure that it is equipped to admit only what is beneficial, and to exclude all that is harmful. To wash, for instance, contributes to our physical health and well-being. But if we have the right mental attitude when washing we can also absorb other forces and currents that keep us in touch with the life of the cosmos. The skin possesses an array of antennae and radar systems by means of which we both emit and absorb fluidic influences. From time immemorial magicians and sorcerers, who knew about these things, have performed their magic rites in the nude, for in this way they were more sensitive to the invisible influences of the spirits, and better able to project forces in order to work their will on people or objects.

There are also magical practices which consist in smearing the body with certain ointments that affect the nervous system and cause a person to leave their physical body and travel through space. It is now known that many so-called witches who claimed to have been present at a sabbath had actually done no more than smear their bodies with certain substances, which, when absorbed by the skin, caused them to disassociate. Their claim to have been present at the sabbath was true, therefore, but they were present and took part in the orgies not in their physical bodies, but in their astral bodies.

Unfortunately, human beings are always ready to experiment with things that put them on the path to hell. They are far less inclined to learn how to communicate with divine forces in an effort to be uplifted. You must understand that when I speak of phenomena of this kind, therefore, it is simply in order to inform you of what exists. It is certainly not my intention to encourage you to take an interest in such practices or to try any dangerous experiments.

Whether they realize it or not, human beings attach considerable importance to the skin. How many wars have been fought—and are still being fought—because of the colour of peoples skins, black, white, yellow or red! The fact that all other aspects of the body are the same, with the same forms and the same functions, is secondary. It is the skin that counts. The skin—which does not usually interest people so much, except when it comes to applying lotions, beauty creams, or make-up— suddenly acquires capital importance, and men and women start to massacre each other because of its colour. But they would do far better to forget about the colour of the skin and pay more attention to keeping it in good condition so that it can fill its role as a protection and as an instrument of perception. What an extraordinary thing the skin is—so delicate and flexible, and at the same time so strong. And when it has been torn or damaged it heals itself so quickly. The Egyptians, who embalmed the dead, have shown us how tough the skin can be, for in certain conditions it can last for hundreds and thousands of years.

In giving us our skin, cosmic intelligence has given us a sense organ whose functions extend even to the spiritual plane. It is important to know that the skin produces subtle secretions which eventually endow it with certain properties, and if we do not want to destroy this etheric film, we have to observe certain rules of life, for everything is reflected in the skin. If we learned to recognize what a person's skin reveals, we would be able to tell exactly his state of mind and his physical condition. A person's skin can be healthy or anaemic, intelligent or stupid, lazy or active. And, of course, this varies according to circumstances. One day their skin might be alive and radiant, and the next drab and lifeless. The same can be said of hair, for it is made of the same elements as the skin. It too reflects both one's physical health and the state of one's inner life.

By looking at people's skin it is possible to tell exactly what kind of lives they lead. A gross, materialistic life or a truly spiritual life is immediately reflected in the texture and colour of the skin. And it is also interesting to note that a person's skin is not the same in every part of the body. In some places it is smooth and finely textured, in others there may be wrinkles or blemishes. One even sees people whose skin, although quite white, seems to have blue, mauve, or yellow undertones. This shows that behind the visible facade of the skin, there are other skins which cannot be seen but which radiate particles that may be pure or impure, luminous, colourful or drab. A very long time ago I met a woman in Zurich who was clairvoyant, and the thing that struck me most forcibly about her face, and which I have never forgotten, was her skin, the sanctity of her skin. It was this that convinced me that she was a truly great clairvoyant.

So try to understand in what way you should care for your skin. You can forget about the question of colour. You can also pay less attention to so-called 'skin care' products. Remember instead that the skin is the best garment that heaven has given us and that it can become a veritable organ of knowledge. But before this becomes possible we have to improve the way we live.

Chapter Ten

THE PERFUME OF EDEN

The reason why the skin is such a difficult subject to talk about is that it is directly related to that of nudity. And, as we have seen, many people still feel that it is indecent to talk about nudity, because it touches on the question of sexuality. At the mention of nudity most people do not immediately think of a person's neck, back, arms, or legs, but of their breasts or their sexual organs. There is nothing scandalous about these organs. They are what they are. But it is the use men and women make of them that leaves a stain on them, and even though this stain is not physical but purely etheric, it is this that one senses at the sight of a naked body. This is why it is better to keep these organs covered, for since most people lead lives of disorder and passion, the emanations of their sexual organs are neither beautiful, nor pure, nor poetic.

I have sometimes been asked what I think of nudism, or of the fact that people on the beaches in summer wear less and less. I remember talking to you one day about my visit to a nudist camp—I had accepted the invitation on the understanding that I could keep my own clothes on—and I must say that it was an interesting experience. Before going, I had wondered what my reactions would be, and to be frank, I must admit that they were quite unexpected. The sight of all those naked bodies gave me a slight feeling of indigestion.

Nudists have instinctively discovered the benefits of a natural way of life, but as they have no initiatic knowledge they do not actually get any great advantage from it. You might think that an initiatic teaching is not necessary in order to know how to expose one's body to sunshine and fresh air. That is true, but if you know nothing about the influences you are exposing yourself to you will not benefit greatly from them. Nudists should have at least a few methods at their disposal and know in what state of mind they should be when exposing their bodies to the sun.

This is important, for what a person receives in this way depends on the nature of their thoughts and feelings. The skin itself is neutral, it absorbs anything, whether good or bad, but its work can be controlled and determined by your consciousness, your thoughts. Depending on what goes on in your mind, your skin will facilitate or obstruct the absorption of certain elements. If your thoughts are pure, luminous and godly, it is as though your skin received orders from above to repulse all poisonous elements and attract only energies and particles that can vivify you. When it is practised in the right conditions this communion with the forces of nature can indeed renew and regenerate you.

But is this what people are really seeking when they go to a nudist camp or the beach? They eat anything, drink alcohol, smoke, take drugs, and have no control over their thoughts and feelings. They are simply there, content to live a purely vegetative or biological life. In such conditions what can you expect their skin to emanate? Nothing but noxious fumes, and those fumes are immediately absorbed by all those around them. Even from a distance one can sense this. In fact I have experienced this several times without even going on to the beach. Walking along the road above the beach I could sense the rank fumes that rose from all those bodies stretched out on the sand. And the astral fumes are often far worse than the physical. You must not conclude that I say this because I do not love human beings. I do love them, and my one desire is to help them, but I cannot avoid seeing and smelling the foulness that emanates from so many of them because of the gross impurity of the way they live.

If they lived intelligent, pure, sensible lives men and women would be like flowers, for the skin is capable of distilling a scent similar to that of certain flowers that one finds only in the mountains. Long, long ago the first man and woman possessed this scent, particularly Eve, and it was because of her scent that plants knew and loved her. She was able to communicate with all the flowers in the Garden of Eden, with the whole vegetable kingdom. No flower exhaled a more exquisite scent than that of Eve. After she committed the original sin—which was a descent into the denser regions of matter—Eve lost her ability to distil this perfume, and the flowers no longer recognized her. For flowers are pure and chaste. They have no astral desires, and when they saw how Eve had sinned they stopped sharing their virtues with her.

It is because women still have the subconscious memory of their original condition in paradise that they feel the need to use perfume. They should know that even now they could distil that perfume if they regained their original state of purity, and they can do this through the purity of their thoughts and feelings and of the food they eat. Yes, the purity of one's food is also very important.

It is not enough to expose one's body to the sun and fresh air. Nudism must be understood quite differently. It should be not only an entirely new conception of things, but it should be accompanied by the relevant discipline, so that human beings may be beautiful and expressive on both the physical and the psychic planes. Otherwise, what is the point? It is better to be clothed. There is something nauseating about the sight of a naked body which is not particularly beautiful and from which emanate unhealthy fumes. A new culture is necessary if there is to be a new humanity. Who will prepare this new culture? Mothers could if they decided to learn and to work with their thoughts and feelings so as to bring healthy children into the world, children who are psychically and physically well-balanced.[1]

Nudism will really come into its own only when human beings realize that they have a great deal of work to do to become beautiful, to perfect themselves. In the meantime, clothes at least have the merit of concealing their imperfections. You may say that they also contribute to perpetuating those imperfections. Yes, in a way that is true. In any case, many people use clothes as a way of concealing their true selves. One senses that they rely on their clothes to create a specific impression of themselves and discourage others from looking any further. But even if they succeed in deceiving

[1] See *Hope for the World: Spiritual Galvanoplasty*, Izvor Collection No. 214.

others, how long will they be able to keep up the pretence for themselves?

There is nothing wrong in the growing tendency among human beings to expose their bodies, but before this becomes a general practice a great many things still need to be improved. At the moment conditions are so far from perfect that it is better for people to be clothed and work on their inner nudity, that is, on acquiring the mastery of their instincts, passions and desires. In this way they will become so pure and luminous, above all they will exhale such exquisite perfume, that when the day comes for them to expose their nudity before the world, the whole of creation will be struck with awe and wonder, sensing something divine that emanates from them as in the far-off days of Eden.

Believe me, the one thing I have really understood, the one thing that has real value for me is life, a life purified and made luminous by those who understand that the reason for their presence on earth is to work to make their whole being a reflection of the divine world.

Chapter Eleven

'IN SPIRIT AND IN TRUTH'

The principles that govern the universe are like the numbers from zero to nine, which constitute the basis for all numerical combinations. Principles, like the first ten numbers, are immutable, but no one can calculate the number and variety of combinations and permutations that can be drawn from them, for they are infinite. This is what we have to learn as time goes on: the new combinations and new forms engendered by the eternal, immutable principles. Movement is a law of life which applies in every area. This is why it is such a mistake on the part of religion to try and make forms last for ever. Only principles are eternal; forms have to change.

One of the most remarkable incidents related in the Gospels is that of the encounter between Jesus and the Samaritan woman who had come to draw water from the well.

Then cometh he to a city of Samaria, which is called Sychar, near to the parcel of ground that Jacob gave to his son Joseph. Now Jacob's well was there. Jesus therefore, being wearied with his journey, sat thus on the well: and it was about the sixth hour.

There cometh a woman of Samaria to draw water: Jesus saith unto her, Give me to drink. For his disciples were gone away unto the city to buy meat. Then saith the woman of Samaria unto him, How is it that thou, being a Jew, askest drink of me, which am a woman of Samaria? for the Jews have no dealings with the Samaritans.

Jesus answered and said unto her, If thou knewest the gift of God, and who it is that saith to thee, Give me to drink, thou wouldest have asked of him, and he would have given thee living water.

The woman saith unto him, Sir, thou hast nothing to draw with, and the well is deep: from whence then hast thou that living water? Art thou greater than our father Jacob, which gave us the well, and drank thereof himself, and his children, and his cattle?

Jesus answered and said unto her, Whosoever shall drink of this water shall thirst again: But whosoever drinketh of the water that I shall give him shall never thirst; but the water that I shall give him shall be in him a well of water springing up into everlasting life. The woman saith unto him, Sir, give me this water, that I thirst not, neither come hither to draw.

Jesus saith unto her, Go, call thy husband and come hither. The woman answered and said, I have no husband. Jesus said unto her, Thou hast well said, I have no husband: For thou hast had five husbands; and he whom thou now hast is not thy husband: in that saidst thou truly. The woman saith unto him, Sir, I perceive that thou art a prophet. Our fathers worshipped in this mountain; and ye say that in Jerusalem is the place where men ought to worship.

Jesus saith unto her, Woman, believe me, the hour cometh when ye shall neither in this mountain, nor yet at Jerusalem, worship the Father... But the hour cometh, and now is, when the true worshippers shall worship the Father in spirit and in truth: for the Father seeketh such to worship him. God is a spirit: and they that worship him must worship him in spirit and in truth.[1]

'Woman, believe me, the hour cometh when ye shall neither in this mountain, nor yet at Jerusalem, worship the Father... But the hour cometh, and now is, when the true worshippers shall worship the Father in spirit and in truth.'

[1] John 4, 5-24

The extraordinary thing about this scene is that
Jesus revealed these things to a woman who was
obviously quite incapable of understanding what he
was saying. After all, one can hardly hold it against
her when one considers that for centuries many of
the greatest theologians have also failed to
understand their true significance.

'The hour cometh when ye shall neither in this
mountain, nor yet at Jerusalem, worship the
Father...' Jesus gives no indication of a holy place
that is destined to supplant the mountain of
Samaria or the temple of Jerusalem. Instead of a
place he mentions two of the most abstract words
known to man: spirit and truth. The spirit as
opposed to matter. Truth as opposed to falsehood,
error, illusion, and superficial appearances. To
worship God in spirit means to discard the material
forms that shackle us and prevent us from moving
freely; to worship in truth means to shed our
attachment to illusion and external appearances.

Some might say that the words 'in spirit and in
truth' define Christianity, the religion of Jesus, and
set it apart from both the religion of Moses and the
pagan religions that abounded in Palestine at the
time. But I do not agree with this. For one thing
Christianity has retained many traces of Judaism—
and even of those pagan religions—in its beliefs,
rites, and shrines. Also, all religions have a
tendency to crystallize, and to be attached to

material forms and external practices. When Jesus said that God must be worshipped in spirit and in truth he was presenting this as an ideal for all religions. If he came back today he would certainly say much the same thing: 'The time has come to worship God neither in Jerusalem, nor in Rome, nor in Mecca, nor at Banaras, but in spirit and in truth.'

Jesus had many revolutionary ideas, but that did not mean that he had no respect for the precepts of Moses and certain aspects of the old order. On the contrary, for he also said, 'Think not that I am come to destroy the law, or the prophets: I am not come to destroy but to fulfil. For verily I say unto you, Till heaven and earth pass, one jot or one tittle shall in no wise pass from the law, till all be fulfilled.' Jesus' only desire was to lead human beings further on the path of true religion.

A spiritual master has exactly the same objective as any other teacher: he has to help human beings to advance, just as a teacher helps his pupils. He knows that many will be incapable of following him, for his ideas and recommendations will be too advanced for them, but does this mean that he should neglect the few who are capable, and who want to advance? Should he leave them to stagnate? No, why should he take the lowest common denominator, the weakest and least capable as his norm? A master must keep urging human beings forward, but at the same time he must be very understanding and sympathetic with those who are not really capable of doing more for the moment.

Jesus looked for a way of teaching that would touch both the simple folk, the crowds that gathered round him, and those who were more advanced spiritually. This is why he taught in parables. One day, when his disciples asked him: 'Why do you speak to them in parables?' he replied, 'Because it has been given to you to know the mysteries of the kingdom of Heaven, but to them it has not been given.' When speaking to the masses he used stories and analogies; when he spoke to his disciples he explained how to interpret those stories and analogies in relation to the virtues. And from among his disciples he chose one in particular, St John, to whom he revealed the underlying meaning of his words. In other words, he gave the form of his teaching to the masses, the content to his disciples, and the meaning to St John.

This has always been the pattern: the masses see no further than the form; disciples work with the content; and initiates reach the meaning, the essence of which is summed up in these two words, spirit and truth. What clearer indication could we have that in Jesus' teaching there is also an esoteric dimension? And it is fortunate that he said this, for it would be virtually impossible to find a similar mention anywhere in the Gospels. One even wonders how it is that this particular passage has survived when so many others have been deleted or transformed.

When you want a child to understand something you have to use stories and pictures or objects. Where religion is concerned most human beings are still children. They need something concrete and tangible to hang on to. Imagine how the faithful of the world's religions would feel if they were told one day that there would be no more churches or temples or synagogues, no more religious ceremonies, no more statues or pious pictures, no more clergy; that every material, external manifestation of religion would disappear because the time had come to worship God in spirit and in truth. They would feel utterly lost, as though they had nothing to hold on to any more. Only someone who is exceptionally highly evolved is capable of finding within his own soul and spirit the sanctuary in which he can communicate with the Lord, in which he can touch and taste and breathe the splendours of heaven. Of course, such an expansion of consciousness is highly desirable. Those who achieve it are free from all limitations, for the world of the soul and spirit is vaster and more beautiful than any other. In that world they

are free to work without restrictions to build a
future for themselves as sons and daughters of God.

In the meantime, however, as we are still on
earth, we are obliged to express our beliefs in
concrete forms. Places of worship, liturgical
objects, the religious feast days that punctuate the
weeks and months of the year... all these are the
concrete expression of our religion. But they are
only an expression. They are not the religion itself.
You cannot squeeze the Deity into a church,
temple, or synagogue, or into an object, even a
host. To claim that this is possible is to disparage
God. Believe me, I have no desire to offend
Christians, but I have to say that although the
notion that it is sufficient to swallow a host in order
to communicate with Christ is a magnificent
invention, it is still an invention.

How can anyone imagine that Christ, the Son of
God, would allow any priest, however worthy or
unworthy, to shut him up in a host? What do they
take him for? And they call this the mystery of the
Eucharist! But there is no mystery here, only a
spiritual reality that is governed by certain laws. It
is true that certain fluidic influences can be
enclosed in an object, but not God. Besides, Jesus
did not say, 'He who eats me... who drinks me.' He
said, 'He who eats my flesh and drinks my
blood...' In other words, it is not Christ who is
eaten or drunk; it is something which belongs to

him, but which is not him himself. The body and
blood of Christ are cosmic elements that can be
absorbed by eating and also by breathing and
meditating, and they can also be condensed in an
object. But no one can lay hold of Christ himself,
of the spirit of Christ.

You cannot live a religion in spirit and in truth
if you continue to cling to the things that are down
here, close to hand—or to your mouth. You have to
move to a higher plane, for Christ is to be found on
a very, very high plane. If you want to drink the
purest water you have to climb the mountain and
drink at the source. If you are incapable of reaching
the source you will have to drink the polluted water
of the streams below, and then, of course, you will
catch their microbes.

Do not misunderstand me, I am not against
Communion. I am not saying that you should not
take part in the Eucharist. I am simply saying that
you must see things in the right perspective. It is
inaccurate to say that a priest changes the bread and
wine into Christ. You cannot help people to reach a
better understanding of the spiritual life by
convincing them that the best way to be in touch
with the Deity is through the bread and wine. Why
try to depreciate God by locking him up in
something material? Why mislead human beings
with all these false beliefs? Think of all the
millions of men and women who know nothing

about the Christian Communion: have they no hope of being in communion with the Lord just as well and as truly as Christians? Do you think that in order to be in touch with God they must become Christians? God bless my soul! Why restrict yourselves—and try to restrict others—in this way?

Human beings have always felt the need to force their own views on others and limit their freedom of action. And this tendency has often led to extremes. In some cultures, for instance, it has led to the deformation or mutilation of people's physical bodies by binding the feet or elongating the skull. But in every country and in every area of life there are those who seek to impose physical or psychological constraints on others.

Now I ask you, what do Christians say about the fate of the billions throughout history who have never heard of the Mass or of Communion? Will God reject them? When you think about this, is it not obvious that communion has to be understood in a much broader sense? Communion is an essential condition of life. The only question is how we communicate? And the answer is that we communicate in any number of ways, beginning with the food we eat every day; for although food is material, the life of the Creator impregnates it, and through a conscious work of the mind we can learn to absorb immaterial elements from it with which to nourish our soul and spirit. True communion is this, the nourishment of the soul and spirit.

When breathing, sleeping, gazing at the beauties of nature—mountains, the sea, the stars, or the sun—it is possible to experience moments of an exalted state of consciousness which are a true communion, the only true communion that gives meaning to the Communion of Christians. To take the bread and wine will do nothing for you if you have not learned to communicate with the Creator in a more profound and far-reaching way through all the ordinary acts of your daily life—eating, drinking, moving about, breathing, looking, listening, sleeping, loving, and working.

Naturally, if you prefer to stick to the poorer and more limited conception of communion you are free to do so. But one day you will be forced to give it up. If not today, in the future, for Jesus' prophecy must be fulfilled. Even if you refuse to accept these truths from me, heaven will send others who will say the same thing.

It is not a question of belonging to one religion rather than to another, of observing certain rites and practices rather than others. A rite, after all, is only a form, and a form is useful only insofar as one is capable of animating it, of giving it a content.

There is a tale I heard when I was young, in Bulgaria. It was about a bishop who was travelling with his retinue. Early one morning they hired a boat to take them over a lake, but before they got to

their destination a storm got up and the boat was
driven on to a lonely stretch of coast. While they
were thanking God for saving them from great
danger, the bishop saw a young boy coming
towards them, driving his goats.

'Where are we?' asked the bishop. 'What is
your name?'

When the boy answered, the bishop was very
struck by his voice and the purity of his face, and
he asked:

'Do you pray to God, child?'

'Oh, yes!'

'What prayers do you say?'

'Oh,' replied the boy, 'I don't say any prayers.'

'But you just told me that you prayed,'
exclaimed the bishop. 'How do you pray?'

Without a word the boy laid his stick across two
large stones and started to jump back and forth over
it. The bishop and his staff could only look on in
astonishment as the boy, his face shining with joy
at being privileged to show such distinguished
people how he prayed, jumped and jumped until he
was out of breath. When he finally stopped his face
shone with such light that the bishop remained in
thought for a moment before saying:

'That is very good. But there is a better prayer
than that. Would you like to learn it?'

'Oh, yes!'

'Very well, kneel down and repeat after me,

"Our Father, which art in heaven, hallowed be thy name…".'

The boy repeated the words several times, very carefully and with great respect, and the storm having abated, the bishop and his staff prepared to continue their journey. Before leaving, the bishop blessed the young boy and told him to recite the prayer he had taught him every day. A few minutes later, when the boat was already quite a long way from the shore, the bishop saw the boy running towards them on the water, crying out:

'Sir Bishop, Sir Bishop, I have forgotten some of the words of the prayer you taught me.'

'Oh my child,' replied the bishop, awestruck at the sight of such a miracle, 'It does not matter. Pray as you like. The Lord has already heard your prayer.'

Is this a true story? Well, even if it is not, whoever made it up understood that the essence of prayer is not in the form, the words, or the physical attitude of the one praying, but in the intensity of his inner life.

'Neither in this mountain, nor in Jerusalem…' said Jesus, because the virtue of prayer does not depend on where you are. The only thing that counts is you yourself, your own inner temple. You can be praying in the most beautiful sanctuary in the world, but if your inner sanctuary is not pure God will not hear your prayer. If you purify and illuminate your inner sanctuary, on the other hand, no matter where you are your prayer will rise to the throne of God.

Just as there is no special place to worship God in spirit and in truth, neither is there any special time. Why do the different religions set aside a particular day for worship? Muslims have chosen Friday, the Jews Saturday, and Christians Sunday. But there is no real difference between any of these days. In the eyes of God all days are equally sacred, equally blessed. What an aberration to think that you can devote six days of the week to your ordinary, material concerns, and on the seventh day turn to God! Would you be in any state to appear in the presence of God if you had just spent six days living without rhyme or reason? Do you think that God appreciates this kind of hypocrisy? Make no mistake about it, the way you live on the seventh day will be determined by the way you have lived on the previous six days. When you live in Christ's religion, in spirit and in truth, wherever you may be and whatever the day of the week, you will always be in God's temple. It will always be the right time and place to praise and worship him.

Jesus did not destroy the religion of his forebears. He took it to greater heights, and gave it greater depth and breadth. And what about myself? Do I want to destroy Christianity? Absolutely not!

What I want is to do, and think, and feel as Jesus thought, and felt, and did. And if I have still not achieved this, I can at least continue to hope and work to that end.

Chapter Twelve

AN IMAGE CAN BE
A SUPPORT FOR PRAYER

At various periods in the course of history there have been iconoclasts: convinced believers who had no doubt meditated to such good effect on Jesus' words about worshipping God in spirit and in truth that they tried to forbid the use of statues and sacred images. The result was that they met with violent opposition from those who clung to their images, and much blood was spilt. The attitude of the iconoclasts was false. Why should we discard all images? The real question is not whether to keep or discard them, but what attitude to have towards them. Initiates have a very wise attitude in this regard. They do not need churches or temples in which to worship, they do not need statues or icons, but when they enter a sanctuary of any kind they show respect to these things, because they know that they are vehicles of a vast pedagogical science. An image or statue is not an end in itself. It is no more than an instrument, a support for thoughts and prayers. And this applies not only to sacred images, but to everything that exists.

A very simple example will help you to understand this, the example of the telephone. Suppose someone has never seen a telephone in his life and has no idea what it is for. He sees you pick up an object and put it to your ear, tap on a series of little buttons, and then start shouting, 'You idiot! What made you do that? I'll murder you!' Or perhaps he hears you saying gently, 'Hello darling! How are you? Oh, how good it is to hear your voice. I love you.' The onlooker would be sure that you had taken leave of your senses: 'He's crazy,' he would say. 'Listen to him. He is talking to an object, cursing or whispering sweet nothings at it. He should be locked up!' Do you understand? Have you ever thought about what a telephone can teach you? You use it, but you never think about it. What is there to understand in a telephone? Just this: you use a telephone to talk, not to the phone, but to someone else, someone who is in another place, perhaps very far away. And that person hears and answers you. In other words, you use this inanimate object to communicate with other living beings.

You are well aware that it would be ridiculous

to address words of endearment to the phone itself, and yet, in other circumstances you do exactly this: you focus on objects or beings without realizing that their only purpose is to serve as intermediaries between you and other beings or objects. Now if we apply this to the realm of religion, we can say that this is the proper function of relics, which have played such a prominent part in the history of Christendom. Any relic can be precious, as long as you have the right attitude towards it. Relics contain many things, but they do not contain the living being you want to get in touch with. A relic is simply a kind of clue, a support on which to hang your quest.

It is not wrong to be attached to an object. It can even be useful, as long as you do not stop there, as long as you take it as a starting point for meditation. Through meditation you can go beyond the material object and reach an inner state of mind that enables you to relate to the absent being it represents. Magic—what is known as natural magic—is based on the principle that physical objects can be used to establish a relationship with beings and forces of the spiritual world. It is in this that natural magic differs from divine magic, or theurgy, which uses only names and numbers, immaterial principles. Of course, material supports are not indispensable in order to get in touch with heavenly entities. Initiates, for instance, no longer need them. But before reaching this advanced stage ordinary human beings need the help of concrete, tangible objects. In fact, this is why we are all on earth. We have to start by touching and tasting things; then we have to learn to see, and hear, and breathe them. Finally, we have to sense and understand them. Through sensation and understanding we reach the spiritual world.

One day, when I was very young, in Bulgaria, I was breathing the scent of a rose (it is true that the perfume of Bulgarian roses is unrivalled), and I suddenly felt myself leaving my physical body. I seemed to fly out into space, and there I discovered a new world of light and beauty. After that I often tried to repeat the experience. Thanks to the quintessences that imbue it, the perfume of that rose, the rose itself, brought me into contact with beings that have been with me ever since. On that occasion I found that I learned a great deal from roses, and they have taught me even more since then. So, as you see, something quite small can reveal something immense.

What is a rose—or even a single rose petal? For most people it is something quite insignificant, but for an initiate who is versed in cabbalistic science it is a means of communication with the world of Venus. Venus belongs to the Sephirah Netzach, and it was Venus that created the rose.

Look at this rose petal. It is impregnated with the pure quintessence of Netzach, and you can use it to make contact with the inhabitants and virtues of that region. Look at it and love it, and it will give you something in return by putting you in touch with the inhabitants of Venus, who are more highly evolved than those of earth. If you need love, tenderness, beauty, and perfume, they can be yours, thanks to this petal. It is simple. It is the principle of magic, both black and white magic. A rose petal is not Venus. You have to go beyond the petal, for it has nothing of its own to give you. Remember simply that even a petal can be an intermediary, a means through which you can communicate with very exalted beings, and they can communicate their gifts to you. In the same way, the statue of a divinity is not the divinity it represents. You may pray to it, but it will not be the statue that helps or protects you. It will simply be a means of getting in touch with the divinity, and in this way all kinds of possibilities will be open to you. Like a rose petal, a statue is no more than a springboard.

What I have been giving you today are some of the basic teachings of initiatic science, and if you apply them, infinite possibilities will open up before you. It is entirely up to you. First and foremost, however, you have to understand. The applications will follow, one after another, once you understand. One day you will taste eternal life if you embrace this philosophy.

As I say, forms are useful, necessary even, but you must not stop there. You must always seek the principle that lies behind them. Only in this way can you obtain the qualities they represent. 'In spirit and in truth' does not mean that we must never seek the support of something material, whether an object or a being, but that we must not be content to stop there and go no further.

In any case, as we can see from history, when people cling to and are content with material forms, it can lead to terrible aberrations. When relics and souvenirs become too important people vie with others for their possession. Think of all that has gone on in Christian countries because of the relics of saints. The greedy and avaricious have built up a flourishing trade, thanks to their popularity. Why were they so sought after? Because great numbers of pilgrims flocked to the sanctuaries that possessed them, and this was good for business. In fact, the demand for relics was so great that many enterprising individuals manufactured false ones.

The story goes that a Russian tsar, having heard that an unidentified monastery possessed the head of St John the Baptist, published a proclamation throughout the land, requesting that the relic be brought to him, to be kept in his chapel. To his amazement, nearly a dozen heads arrived, one after the other, each one of which, it was claimed, was the head of John the Baptist. And then, too, there are all those relics of the cross on which Jesus was crucified: for two thousand years pieces of the 'true cross' have been bought and sold. A whole forest must have been felled to produce so many. Poor, unfortunate human beings! They neglect the living spirit and cling to dead relics... for the delight of swindlers who make money out of them! Really, when one sees the spectacle of certain places of pilgrimage, such as Lourdes, one cannot help wondering...

Or look at Lisieux: shop after shop selling souvenirs of the poor 'Little Flower'! She has become an object of commerce. Yes, all because, instead of teaching Christians where to look for the real Saint Thérèse, some people have preferred to exploit the credulity and naïve faith of others in order to make money. For my part, I am devoted to little Saint Thérèse. In fact, it is precisely because I am so fond of her that I was not content to visit the cathedral in Lisieux or to buy a photograph of her. I did what I had to do to meet her. Yes, she has come to see me more than once, and she has told me many things. You can understand this as you please...

Of course, when someone gave me a hair from the head of Saint Thérèse I did not throw it away.

But was it actually hers, I wonder? It seems to me that all the hairs that are reputed to have come from the head of this or that saint would make a good many wigs. In Bulgaria, when the brothers and sisters found what they thought was one of Peter Deunov's hairs, they would pick it up and treasure it. But what possible benefit is to be gained from treasuring a hair from the head of a saint or an initiate? It is the example and teaching of these beings that we should treasure and follow. We would do far better to leave their hair and all the rest alone.

To worship God in spirit and in truth… This is the ideal proclaimed by Jesus, and because it goes against the material interests of many people they ignore it. But Jesus is still here, still at work, and one day, whether they like it or not, he will oblige such people to change. One day he will come in person to shake them awake, saying: 'You have never tried to find my spirit. You have fallen asleep, content with a few physical relics, and now you are dead, paralysed by sclerosis.' Yes, it is Jesus himself who will come and wake them up.

The extraordinary thing is that, for no other reason than that they possess and venerate a physical object that once belonged to a saint, people see themselves as spiritualists. Far from it! You can claim to be a spiritualist and still behave as a complete materialist. Whether you are a spiritualist or a materialist depends on your level of consciousness. The fact that you are interested in the invisible world does not automatically make you a spiritualist, any more than an interest in the material world necessarily makes you a materialist. It is the way in which you are interested in the spirit or in matter that makes you a spiritualist or a materialist. Religion as it is practised by some people is actually a form of materialism. This is why, instead of criticizing materialists, a great many people should examine their own attitude and see whether, in fact, they themselves are not materialists, since they focus exclusively on the form, and lose sight of the content and the meaning behind those forms. Do you want to be a genuine spiritualist? If so, you must seek the spirit that vivifies and the truth that sets us free.

If you want a picture of a saint to answer your prayers you must not address the picture itself. You must use it as a ladder, as it were, by which to climb up and reach the saint, or even the Lord himself. Every icon, every temple, every created thing is a ladder. The photograph of an initiate or a great spiritual master will be unable to help or to heal you if you do not use it to reach his spirit. This, then, is the true teaching, and it destroys nothing: it constructs. If someone of great spirituality gives you an object that he has blessed, you must not reject it; it is a talisman. But it is no use thinking that it has any intrinsic power of its own. No, you must use it to try and reach much higher, much further, to unite yourself to the cosmic force with which it is imbued. Only in this way can it do you any good.

The initiates do not reject the material world. On the contrary, they enjoy, admire and use all that exists, but they do not delude themselves. They do not confuse the means with the end. They know that the only thing that matters is within man, and that the outer world must be used in the service of the inner world. For light is within, truth is within, peace is within, the kingdom of God is within. It is within ourselves that we must look for these things. All the things we see on the outside are simply the husk of reality, the shadow of reality. In certain circumstances they can be useful and effective, but none of them is absolutely real; they are all destined to crumble and fade away. They are no more than images. Those who cling to them will find not the spirit but matter; not truth but illusion.

Whatever you do, try never to be content with external forms, otherwise you will always be unhappy because your spiritual needs will never be satisfied. Whereas if you get into the habit of seeing the infinite range of affinities and relationships that exist between each form and the divine world, you will go very far. You must all learn to read this book that is lying open before you.

Chapter Thirteen

THE SPIRIT
IS NOT HELD CAPTIVE IN RELICS

The reason why human beings attach so much importance to relics and ruins is that even in the realm of religion they are incapable of detaching themselves from material things. They visit holy places, make pilgrimages, and venerate relics without realizing that it is not by clinging to material vestiges that they will ever be any closer to those who left these vestiges. Instead of finding the spirit they will find only dust and ruins.

A human being consists of a material container or vehicle, the physical body, in which dwell several psychic and spiritual principles. To put this very simply, we say that man is composed of spirit and body, or rather that he is a spirit which inhabits and animates a body. When someone is dead all that remains is the physical body, and even this is soon no more than a skeleton. The spirit is elsewhere. It is no good looking for it in a graveyard; you would soon be obliged to admit that it was not there. You might find a few bones to remind you that a human being had once been there, but that is all. Archeologists sometimes collect fragments of a skeleton and put them in a museum with a label that says, 'Cro-Magnon man', or 'Neanderthal man', and the spirit of that prehistoric man is still alive, still mobile, but it is somewhere else… who knows where?

The same law applies to all that has ever existed on earth. The world is full of vestiges, remains abandoned long since by the spirit. And as human beings are not capable of perceiving and laying hold of the spirit—the instruments that would allow them to do so are not sufficiently developed—they cling to what they can see, the material remains. They go to Egypt, to the foot of the pyramids; to Greece, where they visit Delphi or Eleusis; to India, where they explore the caves at Ajunta or Ellora. The buildings, sculptures, and frescoes in these places inspire them with such awe that they try to recapture something of the spirit that produced these wonders, but it is no longer there.

Christians go to Palestine, to the places where Jesus was born, and where he preached and worked miracles. But although some of the stones may still be the same, the spirit of Jesus is not there. I too have been to Israel, and when I visited the places where Jesus had lived and taught, I took myself back, with all my heart and soul, to those far-off days, but I could sense that the luminous, sacred traces of his presence had all but vanished from the land. For too many centuries too many people have passed through these places, bringing with them so many mundane problems, so many impure and unenlightened thoughts and feelings. You will say that ever since the Middle Ages the Christian churches have done their best to protect the holy places. Yes, by making war on the so-called 'infidels'; by slaughtering and pillaging! A strange way to go about preserving the traces of Jesus' presence!

If we want to preserve the imprint of a great spiritual being we must treat the places he frequented with respect. This is the principal reason for the existence of temples and sanctuaries. At least when people go into such places they do not have the same attitude as in a bar or a dance hall. But it is not enough to refrain from vulgar conversation or noisy laughter. One's inner attitude, thoughts, and feelings are equally important, for it is principally they that leave their mark. As I say, the soil of Palestine has been trampled by too many people who were not animated by Christlike virtues, and the spirit of Jesus has departed.

You must not think that if you visit the holy

places you will find absolutely nothing, no trace of the events that took place or of the people who once lived there. It is always possible to pick up some slight trace. If someone is lost you can sometimes find them with the help of a dog. You let the dog smell a handkerchief or something that belonged to that person, and by following the scent it will sometimes find them miles away. This shows that all human beings leave some trace of their presence, but a trace is not the same thing as the spirit.

There are traces everywhere. The initiates have left traces of their presence in the etheric matter of the places in which they prayed, the temples in which they lived and conducted ceremonies. Certain highly evolved clairvoyants are able to perceive and interpret these traces, and reconstruct the life that went on in the sanctuaries. But even the traces that are found in this way are no more than the husks, the empty envelopes or cast-off garments of the spirit, just as our physical body is the garment of our own soul and spirit. So there is really no guarantee that one will find the spirit when one visits the place where it once breathed.

Where are Jesus and all the other initiates of the past? You may look for them among the ruins of the places they once lived in, and it can happen that if you are in a particularly receptive state of mind you suddenly find yourself in contact with the spirits that once dwelt there, and receive certain revelations from them, but this is extremely rare. If you really want to find traces of Jesus' presence on earth and make contact with his spirit, the spirit that manifested itself two thousand years ago, you must rise to the far-off region known to initiatic science as the Akasha Chronica. This is where the archives of the universe are preserved, and through meditation and contemplation you must endeavour to enter and pursue your research in this sphere. If you are successful you will understand the meaning of the words 'in spirit and in truth'.

Those who study past religions and civilizations investigate the sites of ancient cities and try to interpret every vestige they find, every potsherd, every scrap of cloth or papyrus. And, of course, a great deal of what they discover is very interesting, but it is all incidental. The essential escapes them. If you want to find the spirit of past civilizations and religions there is no alternative, you have to be capable of reaching the cosmic archives, the Akasha Chronica.

Sometimes initiates too study vestiges of the past, because they never neglect or disdain any aspect of creation. But they are well aware that what they are looking at are only clues, indications that something or someone was once there; they are not the spirit. Let me give you another example. I am sure that you have all read the adventures of

Sherlock Holmes. You will remember how he used a trace of cigarette ash, a button, a tiny scrap of mud on the carpet to work his way up a chain of events until he found the criminal. He did not stay in one spot, peering at a clue and surmising about the habits of the criminal; he went and looked for him. And it is this that counts: to move, to go forward. But Christians are content to stay where they are and look no further than the vestiges. They say that they are being faithful to the precepts they have been taught... No, they are being lazy.

Now you are probably wondering how you can communicate with the spirits of the great initiates of India, Egypt, Chaldee, Israel, or Greece? Well, in the first place, they are not dead; they have gone back to where they came from and are now living in their homeland, the sun. Yes, all those luminous spirits who once came to enlighten the world have gone back to live in the sun from which they came, and from this position they continue to help us. It is through the sun's rays that they communicate with us, smile on us, caress, purify, and vivify us. The sun's rays are, as it were, their hands, their arms. But their spirits remain in the sun, and if you succeed in following the traces of the sun's rays you will eventually reach them.

Only the spirit vivifies. Material vestiges are like tin cans of preserves. If you want green peas, sardines, or cherries for lunch you can open some tins and there you are. They are not bad, but there is not the same life in those peas, sardines, and cherries as there would be if they were fresh. I advise you to forget about your tins of preserves and go to the one restaurant where the food is always perfectly fresh. What restaurant is that? The restaurant of the sun. Once you make up your minds to eat regularly at this restaurant you will find yourselves becoming stronger and more enlightened.

You must understand that when I speak of the sun I am not saying that there is nothing higher or more perfect. Even the sun, the physical sun, is a vestige. The only true spirit is the spirit of the sun, but the spirit of the sun is not a prisoner. It is free to go anywhere in the universe. You do not believe me? It is true, you know: the spirit of the sun is not always there. It comes and goes, it travels throughout infinite space, it is everywhere. Are you beginning to understand what region I am leading you to? Perhaps you will protest that it is too far away, and too high up, that it is making your head spin? So much the better! If your head is spinning it means that you are beginning to rise above the earthly abyss.

But let us come down to earth again, for I have something to say about preserves. There is no law against eating tinned food. Sometimes we cannot avoid it, because it would be too complicated to find enough fresh food. In any case, a few tinned peas or sardines have never hurt anyone; I sometimes eat them myself. When I say that you should not eat preserves I am talking about spiritual food. When it comes to spiritual food I tell you frankly, I never touch preserves. I sort out and discard all those stale notions concocted by ignorant human minds. If others take pleasure in eating them that is their business, but for my part I refuse to have anything to do with them. Now please do not go round saying, 'The Master says that you should not eat tinned food.' It is so much easier to talk about tinned foods than to make the effort to understand that what I am saying concerns primarily the spiritual plane.

Continue to visit the places where saints and initiates have lived if you want to, but be sure to keep in mind that the main purpose of these places is to encourage you to seek the one sacred place that is within you. You can visit all the holy places scattered over the face of the earth, but if you fail to find this holy place within, you will sense nothing and find nothing. You will continue to be poor, empty, and dissatisfied. Work, therefore, to create the right inner conditions so that, wherever you are, you will always be in touch with the spirit of all those great beings who have visited the earth, so that you will be nourished by their wisdom and love.

As often happens, this brings us back again to the supremacy of the subjective over the objective. Of course, those who seek truth or happiness outside themselves will always find some degree of satisfaction, a vague reflection, a slight trace, but they will never feel satisfied or inwardly fulfilled for long. It is within yourselves that you must look.

Chapter Fourteen

SPEAK TO THE SPIRIT OF
THOSE YOU LOVE

Let us see now whether we cannot find even broader meaning in Jesus' words 'in spirit and in truth'. Take an example from everyday life that I am sure you have all experienced at some time or another. When a well-loved friend or relation dies they leave you all kinds of souvenirs: books, letters, photographs, clothes, and furniture. You look at these things and touch them with affection, and perhaps you put some flowers or a candle in front of their photograph. To do this is normal, but what are you actually looking for in these souvenirs? Certainly not the spirit of the person you loved. As long as your attention is on these physical souvenirs, you are dealing not with the spirit but with matter. And the same is true when you visit a friend's grave; it is a perfectly normal thing to do, but you will not find him there. He is somewhere else. His body is there, but that is all; his spirit has left this world. And if you really love him and want to find him again, you would do better to go to where he is instead of mourning at his grave, for he is not there; and if you keep trying to find him there you will be holding him back and causing him great suffering. If you really want to find a loved one who has died you must strive to go to where he is, that is, in the realm of the spirit. Unless you do this you will be confining yourself to matter and to untruth.

Some people might say, 'Oh, it is not difficult to get in touch with the spirits of the dead. You only have to go to a spiritualist seance.' But do you really think that you can just go to a seance and say, 'Spirit are you there?' and you will be in touch with the spirit of the person you want? Nothing is less certain. The entities that respond to a medium are often ghosts and elementals of the astral plane, and they are very good at hoodwinking human beings. God is the only who knows where to find the one you are looking for.

Of course, if you want to feed on illusion, you are free to do so. But where such practices as spiritism and channelling are concerned, it is important to know that the quality and authenticity of the messages received from the invisible world depend on your own as well as the medium's degree of evolution. It is human beings who, by the quality of their inner life, attract the attention of a particular kind of entity. The invisible world is exactly like the visible world in that amongst its inhabitants are some who are very highly evolved, and very pure, luminous, and truthful, but there are others who delight in misleading and tormenting human beings, and who are always trying to harm them. Unfortunately, it is often the latter kind of spirit that speaks through the medium during a seance or through table-tapping. How can you expect very exalted entities to put themselves out and be at the beck and call of every nobody who claims to be a medium, just in order to satisfy your curiosity or greed?

Every genuine initiate will say the same thing: when a spiritualist seance succeeds in producing an apparition or materialization, this does not necessarily mean that the medium has managed to make any spirits of light appear. More often than not the apparitions are produced by spirits that are known as shadows, husks, ghosts, or elementals, who take pleasure in deceiving human beings. And this, of course, means that the messages received in such seances are almost always misleading and often completely false.

Human beings constantly venture into the invisible world without really understanding what it is or what kinds of creatures inhabit it. Those who are capable of seeing the reality of the spiritual world are rare. Genuine clairvoyants are very rare, and anyone who is eager to communicate with the spirits should be aware that they are likely to be led astray. They may occasionally receive a correct answer to a question, but even when this happens it is usually a question of chance.

Many of you will probably wonder why heaven allows the forces of the invisible world to mislead human beings. Well, as you know, heaven allows a great many things. For instance, it leaves the creatures that dwell in swamps and in the depths of the ocean free to prey on each other. Ever since human beings left paradise and descended to the darker regions of matter, they have dwelt in this climate of fog and dust, and have been incapable of distinguishing the realities of the invisible world. This is why we can so easily be deceived and misled. Fortunately, there are also luminous spirits who are willing to help us, but ultimately it depends on us. It is our efforts to rise to a higher level and communicate with heavenly entities that will eventually enable us to perceive true reality. This is why, if you want to communicate with the spirits of the invisible world, whether through your own efforts or those of a medium, you must work to develop your powers of discernment, so as to recognize the true nature of the spirits that manifest themselves, and not believe blindly in everything you see or hear. Every message can contain elements both true and false, and you must be capable of sorting truth from falsehood.

You must also realize that if something that has been foretold by a medium fails to materialize, it does not necessarily mean that the medium was mistaken. It may be you yourself who prevents it from happening. Human beings, after all, have their role to play in what happens in the world. To the extent to which they are free, it is they who permit or obstruct events. The invisible world is full of negatives that are just waiting to be developed on the physical plane, and these negatives can be perceived by you or by a medium, but they can also be replaced by other developments formed by yourself, so that events do not conform to what you foresaw. This is why the prophecies of even the greatest clairvoyants do not always come true. If too many human beings oppose them the combined force of their will may constitute an insuperable obstacle to their realization. Only the most basic, essential facts can never be changed.

Genuine messages, predictions, and prophecies are like imprints on the soul of the world, and they can be reflected or transmitted to us quite unwittingly by birds, or animals,   or even by other human beings. A long apprenticeship is necessary before you become capable of deciphering them correctly, but it is not because they are subject to misreading that they should be rejected out of hand.

You must simply examine the messages you receive very carefully, and look to nature, particularly to nature within yourself, to confirm or refute them. In this way, little by little, you will learn to interpret them correctly. In the meantime, concentrate all your energies on achieving your own perfection.

If we are to find our way through the labyrinth of life, we need to know a few rules that have been bequeathed to us by the great masters. Unfortunately, we always have a tendency to take the path of least resistance, and look for easier ways, paths that match our own tastes and desires. It is this tendency that makes us lose our way, for once we allow ourselves to go against the laws, everything in nature contributes to leading us astray. Whereas if we are in tune with the divine laws, if we live and act in harmony with the supreme principle, everything in nature helps, guides, strengthens, and enlightens us.

Think about it carefully, therefore, before calling up the spirit of the dead in a seance. If you really want to get in touch with someone there are other, more reliable and far less dangerous ways of doing so. If the person you want to communicate with possessed great spiritual qualities, he is now in a place of peace, light, and beauty, and the only infallible way of getting in touch with him is to cultivate those same qualities in yourself. Of course, it is much more difficult to do this than to ask a medium to call up his spirit, or to visit his grave, or gaze at his photo while indulging in all kinds of phantasmagoria. But if you truly want to find this person you have no choice. You can only approach him through the law of affinity. By cultivating the qualities he had, you will be in touch with his spirit.

What I have been saying is just one of the interpretations that can be put on Jesus' words, 'in spirit and in truth'. For these words apply to more than the purely mystical life. They apply to every area of life. Also I would like to add that it is not necessary to wait for those we love to be dead before trying to communicate with their spirit. We should begin already while they are alive—in fact, even more so while they are alive.

Why do most love affairs end badly, in disillusionment and regret? Love is the one thing that men and women value above all else. They all dream of finding the perfect love that will last for ever, and yet when they do find love it is all they can do to make it last for a few years, or a few months. Why? Precisely because they have never understood what 'in spirit and in truth' means. When a man finds himself in love with a woman, or a woman with a man, they look no further than the individual. They do not realize that what makes them love each other is that each is a channel for the beauty, charm, and virtues of another world. They both focus all their affection on one human being and expect him or her to fulfil all their needs. This is a tragic mistake, and it is the source of endless suffering and disappointment. When people do this they are behaving like the man who did not know that the telephone was simply a means of communication and not a living being, or that the deity he invoked was not actually in the statue that represented it.

You find this surprising perhaps, but it is important to understand that men and women should see each other not as a source of love, but as a point from which to work back to the true source. Only in this way can they be sure of never being disappointed, for the water—love—that flows directly from the source is always pure, transparent, and life-giving. Otherwise... well I do not need to tell you what happens otherwise; you are only too well aware of all the pain and illusion that love so often entails. Have you not already experienced it for yourselves?

The disappointments and torments of love stem from the fact that human beings have never really understood what happens when they love someone. They need an initiatic teaching that will show them how to look for the underlying principle that animates each human being. Guided by this initiatic teaching, men will learn to see the eternal feminine principle, the divine Mother, in every woman. And as the divine Mother contains an infinite wealth of colour, perfume, form, and movement, their souls and spirits will never weary of her treasures. The same applies to women, of course. Women must learn to see in every man a channel, a means of reaching the eternal masculine principle, the heavenly Father, and communicating with his wisdom, power, and majesty.

As long as men and women seek no more than the person they love, they will know nothing but frustration. No woman can give a man everything he needs. No man can give a woman what she needs. A man should say, 'My darling, you must realize that it is not I who can make you happy. Even if I gave you all that I possess you would not be satisfied, for your heart is so immense that the universe itself could not fill it. And your mind needs a light that I do not possess. Only God can give you everything. All I ask is that you use me as a means to come closer to God. That is what would make me happy. I shall always be with you, but it is God that you must look for through me.' This is what men and women should say to each other, instead of continually making false promises. But to be capable of saying this implies a whole new education.

Even if you feel that to love in this way is still beyond you, it is important to understand that higher forms of love do exist, and that if you want to be truly happy in your love, you should strive towards these higher forms. For when you love in this way, love will never abandon you; it will be always in your heart, always within you as a state of mind that nothing can disturb or destroy. And to experience love as a constant, unassailable state of mind is to feel an inner glow of warmth and light that never leaves you. Whereas the other kind of love is a brush fire that blazes briefly and leaves you nothing but ashes, darkness, and cold.

When you understand the full compass of the words 'in spirit and in truth' you will go directly to the source for the love that you are now looking for in the physical body of the man or woman you love. Then at last you will find true happiness. As you see, the horizons opened up by these words are vast.

Chapter Fifteen

THE SUN,
THE QUINTESSENCE OF RELIGION

In every country I have been to I have visited the churches, temples, basilicas, mosques, and pagodas. Yes, for I do not despise these sacred places; on the contrary, I have always made a point of visiting them and praying in them.

The question we should ask ourselves, however, is this: can any temple built by human hands be compared to the universe, this great temple that was created by God? Can there be any sanctuary more sacred than that which was built by God himself? How could anyone imagine that a building made of unstable, destructible materials was more magnificent than the work of God's hands, which it is beyond the power of man to destroy? Why do we always have such a narrow view of things? Let us respect man-made temples, by all means. Let us go and pray in them, but let us understand that we can also worship God in the temple of nature. Especially in the pure, limpid light of morning, when the rising sun appears and shines in this great temple like a glorious host, showering blessings of light, warmth, and life on all created beings.

Is it not magnificent that wherever we are on earth the sun always shines overhead? We never need to travel or make a pilgrimage to find him. The reality of his inexhaustible light, warmth, and life are worth far more than the dubious authenticity of some relic of the cross of Jesus, or a hair or scrap of clothing reputed to have belonged to some saint.

Everything that makes an appearance on earth ends by dying and disappearing. The only thing that never changes is the sun in the heavens, and it is to the sun that we should look for the truth. For when we seek truth we must turn to what is permanent and unchangeable. Unfortunately, human beings either neglect the sun altogether or exaggerate its role. They either think that it has nothing to do with religion or they treat it as a god. And they are wrong in both cases. If they refuse to give the sun a place in their inner life they are depriving themselves of something essential. On the other hand, if they treat it as an idol they are reverting to the mentality of primitive peoples who worshipped the forces of nature. The sun must be simply a means that enables us to find God, our inner sun. When we contemplate the sun, expose ourselves to its rays, and identify with it every day, light, warmth, and life continually grow within us.[1]

This is the fundamental difference between our teaching and the majority of solar religions that have come and gone throughout the history of humanity—and which certainly exist even today in some parts of the world. A good many people, who are unwilling to think about this seriously, seek to amuse themselves and relieve their boredom by laughing at us and calling us sun-worshippers. Well, they can think and say what they please. That is their business. But for those of you who want to understand I repeat: we do not worship the sun; we worship only God. But you only have to look a little more closely at the symbolism of the sun to see that it is the best representation of God we could possibly have. This is our absolute conviction.

We need to find the sun within us, and this takes practice. For you can look at the visible sun for years and imagine all kinds of things about it, but until you feel it radiating, pulsating, vibrating within you, it will always be something foreign. It will have nothing to say to you. It would even be

---

[1] See *'The Splendour of Tiphareth'*, Complete Works, vol. 10.

pointless to go on looking at it. Oh, you might gain
a little warmth, perhaps, a little more life, a few
vitamins, but you will not find the one thing that is
essential. The one thing that is essential is to
discover your inner sun, for your inner sun is a sign
that God dwells within you, and when you find it
you need no more books or pictures, no more
temples or crosses, not even the sun or the stars in
the sky. For all that you need is to be found within
yourself, in your inner sun.

It is in this sense that I often say that the only
genuine religion is the solar religion. I am not
saying that the other religions are false or bad. No,
but they are true only to the extent to which they
resemble the solar religion. How many religions
there are in the world about which we know
practically nothing! And how many more have
disappeared or will one day disappear! Even the
Christian religion can disappear, but if it takes its
inspiration from the solar religion, it will be born
again in another form, for—although Christians
have never realized this—Jesus' religion was a
solar religion. If the sun were not our model and
example, how could we have any notion of what
Jesus meant when he said, for instance: 'Be ye
perfect as your heavenly Father is perfect'?

If we want to become truly perfect the only
possible being on whom to model ourselves is the
sun. Not the saints. Not the initiates. The saints and

initiates can certainly give us an example of great virtue, but they know very well that they are as nothing compared with the sun. This is why their bearing is always modest and unassuming. They bow before the superiority of the sun. They know that whatever they do their light, warmth, and life can never compare with the light, warmth, and life of the sun.

'If that is true,' you will object, 'how do you explain that Jesus declared himself to be the light of the world?' When Jesus said this he was identifying with Christ, the cosmic spirit that illuminates not only this world, but the whole universe and all its inhabitants. Christ is the true cosmic sun, the true spirit of the sun. In this sense we can say that the physical sun that we see in the sky is the clue, the trace that can lead us to Christ, the cosmic sun. And this means, of course, that we must seek the spirit of the sun, and not be content, in the way of astronomers, with the sun's physical 'carcass'.

This is why, when spring comes around each year, you must prepare to contemplate the sun, knowing that the sun alone is capable of ordering and harmonizing your inner being, and filling you with light, love, peace, and joy. What a privilege to be able to contemplate the sun as it rises every morning! Nothing is more beautiful. It is impossible to tear oneself away from this spectacle of the pure fountainhead, the pulsation and flow of life itself! One is seized by a sense of the sacred, and this is particularly strong if you are present before the sun rises and witness the first light of dawn. You sense that the whole of nature is gathered to celebrate a great mystery. You feel that you even have to walk differently so as not to disturb the atmosphere. This is true poetry, and we should pray that all human beings may one day sense this fullness of life and drink from it.

The sunrise is a symbol, and this symbol is present in every manifestation of life. Everything that progresses, grows, and blooms is linked to the rising sun by a relationship of affinity. What this means to you will depend entirely on your faith and the fervour with which you concentrate on the sun. Depending on your attitude, the sun will either become a powerful, living presence in your life, or it will continue to be no more than a physical object; an object which provides light and warmth, no doubt, but which means no more to you than an electric light bulb or a stove.

Yes, as disciples gradually draw closer to the truth that the sun represents, they begin to find in it a real friend, a friend who speaks to them and on whom they can rely, who will always support and defend them, for the sun alone possesses true strength. This is why it is so important for you to be present at the sunrise every morning, and to learn to look at it with new eyes. Every day you can speak to it in your heart:

'Beloved sun, I have never really known you until now. Of course, I have always seen your great beauty and purity. I have always known that it was you who gave us warmth and light every day, but I never really understood what you were teaching us in this way. Now I know that you are showing me the path of truth, perfection, and fulfilment. My one desire is to be exactly like you.'

Of course, you will never actually be like the sun. That is impossible. But that does not matter; the important thing is to keep the image of the sun in your mind as an ideal, for an impossible ideal is the one thing that can most powerfully act upon, strengthen, and transform a human being. It is not the things you already have and hold, or the successes you have already achieved that are going to help you to evolve further. You must seek the impossible, the unattainable. Only this can incite you to further progress, to constant growth.

Chapter Sixteen

THE TRUTH OF THE SUN
IS IN GIVING

In the Emerald Tablet, Hermes Trismegistus says, 'That which is below is like that which is above, and that which is above is like that which is below.' This means that on earth there must be a visible, tangible expression of the intangible, inaccessible world of truth. It is the sun that is that expression, for truth, like the sun, is what enables us to see things clearly. This is why, of the five virtues—love, wisdom, truth, kindness, and justice—the one that relates most closely to the eyes is truth. You claim to be seeking truth, but can you not see that it is there, before you, in the sun? No, you go on looking for it. The sun goes on shining, and you never even notice that it is telling you: 'Look at me, and try to be like me. I will come and dwell within you, and you will possess truth.'

The sun gives us its light and heat, without

which life cannot exist, and if you want to find truth you too must learn to give. But the giving I am talking about is not a question of bestowing alms in the form of a few pennies, or a crust of bread, or some old clothes. Everything you do can be an occasion for giving, an occasion to be more understanding, more altruistic in your dealings with others; to seek to love rather than to be loved. Those who want to serve will find truth; those who want to be served will never find truth.

Years and years ago, in Bulgaria, while we were in a meeting with the Master Peter Deunov, I remember that he asked us: 'What is the difference between the new teaching and the old?' Some of those present tried to answer, but no one got it quite right. Eventually the Master said, 'The old teaching taught us how to take, and the new teaching teaches us how to give.' What could be more concise or more explicit? Of course, even with such a clear formula, a good deal of explanation is necessary before we really grasp what taking and giving can mean in every area of life.

Kindness, generosity, tolerance, and self-sacrifice are all included in the notion of 'giving'. Selfishness, anger, irritation, jealousy, vulgarity, and a lack of conscience are included in 'taking'. If you observe what goes on around you you will see that those who live in truth can be distinguished from others by their good qualities, particularly by their kindness, selflessness, and greatness of heart. This is why, when I meet someone who claims to possess the truth, but who is aggressive, vindictive, and full of hatred, I feel like telling him to go back to his kennel and keep quiet, for if that is truth, it is not worth making the effort to possess it. But human beings rarely apply these standards. They only have to hear a rabble-rouser preaching hatred and violence in the name of truth, and they are ready not only to follow his philosophy, but to imitate his deeds.

You must never believe those who claim to possess truth unless they can show you their diplomas. 'Their diplomas…' you will say. 'Can you have a diploma for this too?' Indeed you can, but there is a great difference between the diploma I am talking about and one that you get from a college or university. The diploma I am talking about is not printed on a piece of paper, but on a person's very being. It is alive, and initiates and even the spirits of nature can read it from afar, for it shines and radiates light. When one is in the presence of a being who possesses this diploma one feels an influx of light and warmth, as though one were watching the sun rise.

Unfortunately, few human beings have developed the capacity to give. As often as not, when they give someone something, it is only as a preliminary to taking something for themselves.

They are convinced that in order to possess you have to take. But is this necessarily so? An initiate will tell you the opposite: in order to possess you have to give. This needs to be explained. It is true, of course, that you cannot give unless you possess something, and you cannot possess anything if you have received nothing. The great question is from where and from whom you receive. Most human beings go and take what they want from other human beings. They end, in fact, by stealing everything they have—money, strength, ideas, feelings—and the greatest thieves of all are lovers. In fact, as all our poetry, novels, plays, and films are about lovers, you could say that they are all about thieves. They are about those who steal other people's hearts.

All around us, on the physical plane and also on the psychic plane, we see nothing but thievery. Very few human beings think only of giving. And in fact, when these few encounter the opposition and obstruction that is the inevitable lot of those who are idealistic and open-hearted, always willing to welcome and help others, they are tempted to retreat and to decide that it is simply not worth it. If their efforts attract so much hostility what is the good of trying? Well, contrary to all appearances, the effort is well worth it.

You must, of course, realize that it is not because you have a sublime ideal that the rest of the world will necessarily recognize all your efforts, all your good work. On the external plane you will always have unpleasant situations to confront, but on the inner plane you will live in a constant climate of joy. Yes, for a long time you will feel a great difference between the inner and the outer worlds, for not only will there be some who contest and combat what you are doing, but there will also be those who, seeing that you are trying to model yourself on the sun and cultivate the virtues of self-abnegation, generosity, and patience, will hasten to take advantage of you in every way they can. They will do their best to suck you dry and then discard you without a word of thanks. But none of that matters. You must persevere, for perseverance is the only way to safeguard the blessings that flow from your high ideal.

I am sure you often think that your situation is very strange: inwardly you are full of peace, joy, and harmony, while outwardly you are surrounded by opposition and conflict. But this is the way things are at the moment, and given the present state of humanity, it is hard to see how they could be otherwise. This situation is only temporary, however. There is nothing definitive about it. The law of correspondences established by cosmic intelligence is absolute and unassailable, and it means that you will one day receive the reward that exactly matches your thoughts, feelings, desires, and actions. In the meantime, even if you have to suffer the attacks of the world around you, at least you have joy within you.

You will never possess truth until you have pierced all the secrets of the word 'give'. When one sees how people display their acquisitions it is obvious that they are very proud of them, but one day all this stolen wealth will turn to dross. Those who enrich themselves at the expense of others— whether individuals or countries—never really benefit from what they acquire. Sooner or later, even on the physical plane, they are obliged, little by little, to give up their ill-gotten gains.

The chief concern of an initiate is to give. By greeting you, looking and smiling at you, shaking your hand, or talking to you, he gives you something good, something luminous. And in doing so, his own being grows, blossoms, and reaches greater heights of perfection because he is obeying the law of love, and the true law of love is to give. Not to take, to give! At the same time as he gives, though, he also receives, for a stream of pure, transparent light flows to him from the sun.

The Hebrew letter Aleph א is one of the most eloquent symbols of the inner attitude human beings must have if they are to find the right solution to the question of taking and giving. Aleph represents one who has become a link between

heaven and earth in order to receive from heaven
and give to earth. After all, why should anyone
want to take from human beings? The poor
wretches already have so little. Would it not be far
better to take from heaven, whose wealth is infinite,
and give to human beings? Aleph teaches us that
our task is to become a link between heaven and
earth. Symbolically, the link *par excellence*
between heaven and earth is Christ, the perfect
man, for he receives all the treasures of heaven and
pours them out on the earth.

Henceforth, take the letter Aleph as a symbol of
the highest possible ideal. Let it be a constant
reminder of the work you have to do with wisdom
and love. And believe me, you need both love and
wisdom, not only in order to receive blessings from
heaven, but also in order to distribute those
blessings on earth. Love will open your heart both
to heaven and to humanity. Wisdom will teach you
how to relate to the one and the other, for it is not
enough to *want* to relate to both; you also need to
know *how* to do so.

If you study the history of religions you will
find tales of some of those who, in various forms,
have become Aleph. Greek mythology, for
instance, tells of one who is very well known, the
Titan Prometheus, who stole fire from heaven. An
Aleph, that is, a human being whose only ambition
is to give as the sun gives, to bring light and

warmth to others, touches the farthest reaches of space by means of his thoughts and feelings, and in doing so he meets and communicates with a multitude of other beings. For this is what life truly is: a constant, uninterrupted communication with millions of beings.

To resemble the sun... there is no higher ideal than this. Try to nourish this ideal so that it grows and fills you so completely that it inflames and illuminates your whole being. Only this high ideal can awaken the seeds of all that is best within you and cause them to germinate and grow. Without any insistence on your part, without your even thinking about it, you will begin to manifest all these hidden treasures. The only truth worth seeking is this truth of the spiritual sun, which, as soon as it shines within you, causes every good quality to blossom, just as the physical sun brings forth life in the whole of nature.

Chapter Seventeen

THE KINGDOM OF GOD IS WITHIN

It is time today for a thorough re-examination of the beliefs most people hold about God. The notion of a God who never ceases to be angry with his people, who continually threatens and punishes them, or of an old man with a long beard who spends his days scrutinizing and recording their faults was perhaps acceptable in other times and under other conditions. But nowadays these notions seem utterly ridiculous. No one of sound mind would want anything to do with the life and mentality that for thousands of years have been ascribed to God.

Unquestionably, the notion of one single God, introduced by Moses, represented a tremendous step forward in the history of thought. But the time has come for this image of a God of justice—possessive, exacting, vengeful, and merciless—to be revised so that human beings may evolve further. For how can they learn to show patience, tolerance, and goodness towards their fellow human beings if the example before their eyes is of a God forever harsh and unforgiving?

Jesus came to teach humans that God is their father. The emphasis no longer fell exclusively on the notion of justice, but on that of love, kindness, and forgiveness. God was no longer seen as the unyielding taskmaster, before whom human beings could only prostrate themselves like slaves. He was a father, and human beings were his children. This new approach to the relationship between God and humanity gave rise to yet another, even more profound change; one that was revealed in the Gospels, and yet it is still not well understood today. This new perspective concerned the nature of man himself. If God is our father, this means that we are of the same nature as he, for father and child must necessarily be of the same nature. And if we are of the same nature as God, we can identify with him; we are in him and he is in us.

But it is not enough to consider that God is our father and we his children, for in doing so we allow for a separation, a gulf, between us. If he is outside us and we are outside him, it follows that we are at the mercy of whatever exists in the gulf that lies between us, that we are in some way outside and separated from his light, peace, and love.

How many mystics have complained of being forsaken by God! No, God did not forsake them; rather it was they who were unable to keep alive the consciousness of God's presence within them. God never forsakes us. It is in our own consciousness that his presence seems to fade. At times our soul is more receptive, and we feel the inner presence of God's light and warmth. At other times our soul is less open and we feel deprived of his presence. Who is to blame? If you cut yourself off from the sun's rays you will find yourself in the cold and dark. No one says that it is easy to be permanently conscious of the divine presence within us, but this is the end we must work towards by making ourselves a temple of the Deity. Not just a palace, but a temple! To succeed in becoming a palace is indeed no small accomplishment, but a palace lacks the sacredness found in a temple. The Lord will enter and dwell permanently in a human temple. He never forsakes a sanctuary that has been consecrated to him and in which he is worshipped in purity and in light.

Does God exist? And if he exists is he like this or like that? What are we in relation to God? What is the difference between human nature and divine nature? All these questions are pointless. You only need to know that God is not only our creator, but our father, and that we are of the same essence. When Jesus said, 'I and my Father are one,' he was expressing in these few words the greatest mysteries of religion.

Some people will argue that Jesus was truly the son of God, whereas we are only ordinary mortals. Well, this raises a very important question. If Christian theologians chose to consider Jesus as God's equal, as the Christ, the second Person of the Trinity, a cosmic principle, that was their business, but in doing so they created an unbridgeable chasm between Christ and the rest of humanity. Certainly Jesus never taught anything of the kind. He never claimed to be different in essence from other human beings. When he stated that he was the son of God this was not to suggest that he was superior to the rest of humanity. On the contrary, in proclaiming himself the son of God he underscored the divine nature of all human beings. If this were not so, what would be the significance of his injunction to his disciples to 'be perfect, even as your Father who is in heaven is perfect', or of his assurance that 'he that believeth in me, the works that I do shall he do also; and greater works than these shall he do…'?

If Jesus taught that we can do the same work as he did, it means that we are of the same nature, the same essence as he. Why have Christians ignored this aspect of his teaching? As I have said before, it is simply because they are lazy and unwilling to make the slightest effort to follow in his footsteps.

Instead they say, 'As the son of God, Jesus was perfect, and able therefore to manifest extraordinary knowledge, virtue, and power. But we poor miserable wretches are by nature flawed and sinful. It is only normal that we should be weak, selfish, and vicious.' No, it is not normal. Not at all! For we are sons and daughters of God, exactly as Jesus was. The only difference is that Jesus, being conscious of his nature and of the divine work he was destined to accomplish, dedicated his whole life to that work. He had already done a great deal of work in previous incarnations, and came into this world with immense powers and a clear understanding of his mission. But even he had to do a tremendous amount of inner work, including prayer, fasting, and a struggle against temptation. Are you not familiar with the Gospels? Have you never wondered why it was only in his thirtieth year that Jesus received the Holy Spirit? Or why the devil tried to tempt him?

By his example, and the sacrifice of his life, Jesus showed us the path we should take in order, as he said, to do the work that he did. If we are unconscious of this likeness between Jesus and ourselves it is because we have allowed so many foreign elements to obscure and eclipse our divine nature. As a result, of course, we no longer recognize it. But if we work with love and wisdom to purify our thoughts, emotions, and actions, we shall sense this divine nature gradually awakening within us. Yes, the important thing is to achieve a state of consciousness in which we are never again separated from God; in which we know ourselves to be a part of him, to have no existence outside him.

For this is the truth of it: no one can exist if they are separated from God. It is God who created us, who nourishes us, who sustains us in life. There can be no such thing as a creature who is really independent of God. If people feel independent that independence exists only in their minds, for it is possible for human beings deliberately to cut themselves off from their creator. But in doing so they are condemning themselves to spiritual death. You will say, 'But God is in heaven.' Yes, God is in heaven, but is there any reason why we should not, here and now, be in heaven with him?

Do you not see that this is the true religion, the religion of spirit and truth? Until now there has always been a gap, a distance between you and God. And by being outside and apart from God you have actually been outside yourself, outside your true higher self. You have never really found yourself; you are constantly swinging between contradictory states of mind. At one moment you experience inner peace, and have a clear sense of the meaning of your life, and then, without warning, you are thrown into a state of anguish and distress in which everything becomes dark and meaningless. As long as human beings fail to identify with their divine nature they will always be subject to these ups and downs, always hesitant and torn in different directions.

Moses emphasized the fear of the Lord. Since God was seen as an intransigent taskmaster, human beings could only fear him. As the psalmist put it: 'Fear of the Lord is the beginning of wisdom.' But fear is a negative sentiment. Those who always act under the constraint of fear can never really fulfil themselves. In the long run, fear is destructive. With love, on the other hand, a human being can flourish and be fulfilled, and this is why Jesus came to tell us that God is a father. Of course, children are also a little afraid of their father, and that is not a bad thing, for they have to learn that there are rules that must not be broken, and that if they break them they will be punished. But a father is first and foremost someone who is loved by his children, not only because he has given them life, but also because he helps them to reach fulfilment by sharing his wealth with them.

'I and my Father are one.' What immense knowledge we need, what an immense amount of work we have to do before we can say these words! But those for whom this identification is a reality live in absolute fulfilment.

God is within us, just as his kingdom is within us. If you become conscious of being inseparable from the Creator, you will find that you begin to see more and more clearly how to resolve your problems, and particularly how to do good to those around you. Whereas if you feel yourself separated from God you will be left to your own resources. And your resources are very limited. Poor, unfortunate Christians who refuse to tread this path that Jesus opened before them! Let me tell you that many Hindus, who practise Jnana-yoga, the yoga of self-knowledge, and meditate on the words 'I am Him' have a much deeper understanding of these things than Christians. They repeat these words inwardly until they become part of their very flesh and bone, until their puny little self no longer exists. He alone, the Lord almighty, lives in them, and they are capable of working miracles. This is why, when Jesus worked miracles, he would say, 'I can of mine own self do nothing,' and 'Whosoever shall receive me, receiveth not me, but him that sent me.' It is in this sense too that we can say that Jesus was truly the son of God; he was the intermediary between God and man.

If you learn to efface yourself, and melt and merge into one with the Lord, you will become a formidable power, for it is when human beings recognize their insignificance in relation to God that they are truly great. But if you have an inflated sense of your importance, if you behave as though you were the equal of God you will be weak and vulnerable, a nonentity. This is why Jesus said, 'Except you die you shall not live…' In other words, unless you die to your existence as an isolated element separate from the Whole, you will not live with the boundless life of the Whole. The day you succeed in dying to your lower self, it will no longer be you who lives, but the Lord who lives in you. You have to understand these words on the psychic and spiritual plane, otherwise they are meaningless.

The aim and purpose of all spiritual discipline is to come to know oneself as God. This is the meaning of the formula 'I am Him.'

My role is to give you true knowledge, even though I know that at the moment you are not yet capable of putting it into practice. I am obliged to tell you that there is a more perfect way of understanding things, but at the same time I have to be patient and tolerant, and accept the situation as it is today. We must not try to rush things, for they cannot be made to happen prematurely. I think you all know the Gospel parable of the banquet.

A certain man gave a great supper, and bade many: and sent his servant at supper time to say to them that were bidden, Come, for all things are now ready. And they all with one consent began to make excuse. The first said unto him, I have bought a piece of ground, and I must needs go and see it: I pray thee have me excused. And another said, I have bought five yoke of oxen, and I go to prove them: I pray thee have me excused. And another said, I have married a wife, and therefore I cannot come.

The excuses these guests used to justify their unwillingness to attend the banquet are an accurate reflection of the pretexts people give for having no room for God in their lives.

But what if, in their desire to show that they had understood the lesson of this parable, everyone threw over all their social commitments, saying that they had to keep themselves free for the Lord? Obviously, that is not the answer. In fact, it is just as well that many people are not free, for even if they were dedicated to the Lord, too much freedom would simply give them more opportunities to commit errors of judgement. Not everybody is capable of making good use of their freedom. It is far better for some people to be obliged to devote most of their time and energy to their family or profession. If a narrow-minded, fanatical man frees himself from his social obligations in order, as he thinks, to answer the call of the Lord… Well, you can imagine what a disaster it would be. An endless series of blunders!

For the same reason, we cannot expect human beings to detach themselves from all external forms of worship, and to adore God in spirit and in truth before they are ready. Certain things have to change gradually. The fulfilment of Jesus' prophecy is approaching, and for some it has already materialized, but we must understand that a change of such magnitude cannot happen all at the same time for everybody, for it depends on the inner life of each individual.

When something occurs on the physical plane everybody experiences it at the same time. If a government decides to introduce a change in the law, the date when it is to take effect is made public. The decision is made, for instance, to do away with the monarchy and establish a republic, or vice versa, to declare war or to sign a peace treaty, and on a given day all the citizens of the country find themselves in a republic or a monarchy, at peace or at war. Or an Ecumenical Council in Rome decides that as of a certain date the Mass will no longer be said in Latin, and from that day on this ruling is applied. But when Jesus says, 'The hour cometh when the true worshippers shall worship the Father in spirit and in truth,' he is speaking of a spiritual phenomenon, something that affects our inner life and depends for its realization on our degree of spiritual evolution.

Jesus also said, 'The kingdom of God is nigh at

hand.' Many people point out that two thousand years have gone by since he said this, and the kingdom of God seems to be as far away as ever. But they think this because they do not know in what form it is at hand. For some, the kingdom of God has already come; in the hearts and souls of those who were ready to receive it it is already within. For others, it is coming closer. And for still others, it will come some time in the future, but we cannot tell when.

Perhaps you are still not convinced. You cannot help feeling that in view of the efforts that Christians have made over the last two thousand years to bring it about, the kingdom of God surely ought to be here by now. Why are there still so many wars, still so much famine, poverty, and distress in the world? Why? Precisely because human beings have never learned to work in spirit and in truth. They spend their time talking and writing about all the faults and failings of the system—the lack of organization, the incompetence of those in charge, the way good money is thrown after bad, and so on. And thinking to improve the situation, they try to force some to do this, or forbid others to do that, to demote some and promote others, to create innumerable committees and boards of inquiry. The solutions they envisage are always material ones, and their eagerness to impose them leads to endless conflicts. How can the kingdom of God possibly be accomplished in such conditions?

It is time human beings learned to think and behave quite differently. Those who are sincerely anxious to work for the coming of the kingdom must realize that this cannot be achieved with human methods, the methods of matter. It can be achieved only through divine methods, the methods of the spirit. And these methods consist in cultivating the purest and most noble feelings and aspirations, and in using one's power of speech only to express something positive and constructive. It is only by our noble feelings, aspirations, and words that we can attract the attention of luminous powers of the invisible world, and persuade them to come and help us in our work.

Yes, all those of you who harbour the ideal of working for the good of the collectivity must join forces first and foremost in order to do some spiritual work together. It is this spiritual work that will purify your thoughts and feelings and make them so luminous that they will reach out far into space and attract the corresponding entities and elements to come to your assistance. These entities and elements will help you to improve the situation far more effectively than all your criticism and fault-finding, all your plans for reform.

This is the only way to proceed if you want to

apply Jesus' precept to work in spirit and in truth. The lives of those who refuse to accept this teaching will necessarily end in frustration and bitterness, for the thoughts and feelings that constantly revolve in their minds make them prisoners of the lower astral and mental planes. Sooner or later they will be obliged to recognize that all their efforts have been in vain… and this for no other reason than that they did not know how to work. You cannot imagine how many people have given me advice about how to organize the Brotherhood according to their methods, the ordinary methods of the world. But I have never listened to them. I have always worked in the invisible world with the methods of love and light, and today the creations of my soul and spirit are working their way down on to the physical plane, where, little by little, they will all materialize.

'The hour cometh, and now is, when the true worshippers shall worship the Father in spirit and in truth.' 'The kingdom of God is nigh at hand.' These prophecies announce events that are essentially private and inward in nature. Without waiting for them to materialize in the outer world, we must find peace, light, and truth within ourselves, for even if we were to find them in the outer world, we would be incapable of preserving them or even of appreciating them if they were not already established within our own hearts and souls.

By the same author

Izvor Collection
TABLE OF CONTENTS

206 – A PHILOSOPHY OF UNIVERSALITY

1. What is a Sect? – 2. No Church is Eternal – 3. The Spirit Behind the Form – 4. The Advent of the Church of St. John – 5. The Foundations of a Universal Religion – 6. The Great Universal White Brotherhood – 7. For a Universal Notion of the Family – 8. Brotherhood, a Higher State of Consciousness – 9. The Annual Conventions at the Bonfin – 10. The Universal Dimension of All Our Activities.

207 – WHAT IS A SPIRITUAL MASTER?

1. How to Recognize a True Spiritual Master – 2. The Necessity for a Spiritual Master – 3. The Sorcerer's Apprentice – 4. The Exotic Should not be Confused with Spirituality – 5. Learn How to Balance the Material and Spiritual Worlds – 6. A Master is a Mirror Reflecting the Truth – 7. A Master is There Only to Give Light – 8. The Disciple and His Master – 9. The Universal Dimension of a Master – 10. The Magical Presence of a Master – 11. Identification – 12. 'Except Ye Become as Little Children...'

208 – THE EGREGOR OF THE DOVE OR THE REIGN OF PEACE

1. Towards a Better Understanding of Peace – 2. The Advantages of Unity amongst Nations – 3. Aristocracy and Democracy – 4. About Money – 5. The Distribution of Wealth – 6. Communism and Capitalism – 7. Towards a New Understanding of Economics – 8. What Every Politician Should Know – 9. The Kingdom of God.

209 – CHRISTMAS AND EASTER IN THE INITIATIC TRADITION

1. The Feast of the Nativity – 2. The Second Birth – 3. Birth on the Different Planes of Being – 4. 'Except Ye Die Ye Shall not Live' – 5. The Resurrection and the Last Judgment – 6. The Body of Glory.

210 – THE TREE OF THE KNOWLEDGE OF GOOD AND EVIL

1. The Serpent of Genesis – 2. What Good is Evil? – 3. Beyond Good and Evil – 4. Until the Harvest – 5. The Philosophy of Unity – 6. Into the Wilderness to Be Tempted – 7. The Undesirables –8. Suicide is not the Answer – 9. The Real Weapons – 10. The Science of the Initiates, or the Inner Lamps.

211 – FREEDOM, THE SPIRIT TRIUMPHANT

1. Man's Psychic Structure – 2. Mind over Matter – 3. Fate and Freedom – 4. Freedom through Death – 5. Sharing in the Freedom of God – 6. True Freedom: a Consecration of Self – 7. Freedom through

Self-Limitation – 8. Anarchy and Freedom – 9. The Notion of Hierarchy – 10. The Synarchy Within.

212 – LIGHT IS A LIVING SPIRIT

1. Light : Essence of Creation – 2. The Sun's Rays, their Nature and Activity – 3. Gold is Condensed Sunlight – 4. Light Enables us to See and be Seen – 5. Working with Light – 6. The Prism : a Symbol of Man – 7. Purity Clears the Way for Light – 8. Living with the Intensity of Light – 9. The Spiritual Laser.

213 – MAN'S TWO NATURES, HUMAN AND DIVINE

1. Human Nature or Animal Nature ? – 2.The Lower Self is a Reflection – 3. Man's True Identity – 4. Methods of Escape – 5. The Sun Symbolizes the Divine Nature – 6. Put the Personality to Work – 7. Perfection Comes with the Higher Self – 8. The Silent Voice of the Higher Self – 9. Only by Serving the Divine Nature – 10. Address the Higher Self in Others – 11. Man's Return to God, the Victory.

214 – HOPE FOR THE WORLD : SPIRITUAL GALVANOPLASTY

1. What is Spiritual Galvanoplasty? – 2. Reflections of the Two Principles – 3. Marriages Made in Heaven – 4. Love Freely Given – 5. Love on the Lower Plane – 6. Love on the Higher Plane – 7. Love's Goal is Light – 8. The Solar Nature of Sexual Energy – 9. Mankind Transformed – 10. The Original Experiment and the New One – 11. Replenish the Earth ! – 12. Woman's place – 13. The Cosmic Child.

215 – THE TRUE MEANING OF CHRIST'S TEACHING

1. 'Our Father Which Art in Heaven' – 2. 'My Father and I Are One' – 3. 'Be Ye Perfect, Even as Your Father Who is in Heaven is Perfect' – 4. 'Seek Ye First the Kingdom of God and His Justice' – 5. 'On Earth as it is in Heaven' – 6. 'He That Eateth My Flesh and Drinketh My Blood Hath Eternal Life' – 7. 'Father, Forgive Them, For They Know Not What They Do' – 8. 'Unto Him that Smiteth Thee on the One Cheek...' – 9. 'Watch and Pray'.

216 – THE LIVING BOOK OF NATURE

1. The Living Book of Nature – 2. Day and Night – 3. Spring Water or Stagnant Water – 4. Marriage, a Universal Symbol – 5. Distilling the Quintessence – 6. The Power of Fire – 7. The Naked Truth –8. Building a House – 9. Red and White – 10. The River of Life – 11. The New Jerusalem – Perfect Man. I – The Gates. II – The Foundations – 12. Learning to Read and Write.

217 – NEW LIGHT ON THE GOSPELS

1. 'Men do not Put New Wine into Old Bottles' – 2. 'Except Ye Become as Little Children' – 3. The Unjust Stewart – 4. 'Lay up for Yourselves Treasures in Heaven' – 5. The Strait Gate – 6. 'Let Him Which is on the Housetop not Come Down...' – 7. The Calming of the Storm – 8. The First Shall Be Last – 9. The Parable of the Five Wise and the Five Foolish Virgins – 10. 'This is Life Eternal, that they Might Know Thee the Only True God'.

218 – THE SYMBOLIC LANGUAGE OF GEOMETRICAL FIGURES

1. Geometrical Symbolism – 2. The Circle – 3. The Triangle – 4. The Pentagram – 5. The Pyramid – 6. The Cross – 7. The Quadrature of the Circle.

219 – MAN'S SUBTLE BODIES AND CENTRES
the Aura, the Solar Plexus, the Chakras...

1. Human Evolution and the Development of the Spiritual Organs – 2. The Aura – 3. The Solar Plexus – 4. The Hara Centre – 5. Kundalini Force – 6. The Chakras: The Chakra System I. – The Chakra System II. Ajna and Sahasrara.

220 – THE ZODIAC, KEY TO MAN AND TO THE UNIVERSE

1. The Enclosure of the Zodiac – 2. The Zodiac and the Forming of Man – 3. The Planetary Cycle of Hours and Days – 4. The Cross of Destiny – 5. The Axes of Aries–Libra and Taurus–Scorpio – 6. The Virgo–Pisces Axis – 7. The Leo–Aquarius Axis – 8. The Fire and Water Triangles – 9. The Philosophers' Stone : the Sun, the Moon and Mercury – 10. The Twelve Tribes of Israel and the Twelve Labours of Hercules in Relation to the Zodiac.

221 – TRUE ALCHEMY OR THE QUEST FOR PERFECTION

1. Spiritual Alchemy – 2. The Human Tree – 3. Character and Temperament – 4. Our Heritage from the Animal Kingdom – 5. Fear – 6. Stereotypes – 7. Grafting – 8. The Use of Energy – 9. Sacrifice, the Transmutation of Matter – 10. Vainglory and Divine Glory –11. Pride and Humility – 12. The Sublimation of Sexual Energy.

222 – MAN'S PSYCHIC LIFE: ELEMENTS AND STRUCTURES

1. Know Thyself – 2. The Synoptic Table – 3. Several Souls and Several Bodies – 4. Heart, Mind, Soul and Spirit – 5. The Apprenticeship of the Will – 6. Body, Soul and Spirit – 7. Outer Knowledge and Inner Knowledge – 8. From Intellect to Intelligence – 9. True Illumination – 10. The Causal Body – 11. Consciousness–12. The Subconscious – 13. The Higher Self.

223 – CREATION: ARTISTIC AND SPIRITUAL

1. Art, Science and Religion – 2. The Divine Sources of Inspiration – 3. The Work of the Imagination – 4. Prose and Poetry – 5. The Human Voice – 6. Choral Singing – 7. How to Listen to Music – 8. The Magic Power of a Gesture – 9. Beauty – 10. Idealization as a Means of Creation – 11. A Living Masterpiece –12. Building the Temple – Postface.

224 – THE POWERS OF THOUGHT

1. The Reality of Spiritual Work – 2. Thinking the Future – 3. Psychic Pollution – 4. Thoughts are Living Beings – 5. How Thought Produces Material Results – 6. Striking a Balance between Matter and Spirit – 7. The Strength of the Spirit – 8. Rules for Spiritual Work – 9. Thoughts as Weapons – 10. The Power of Concentration – 11. Meditation – 12. Creative Prayer – 13. Reaching for the Unattainable.

225 – HARMONY AND HEALTH

1. Life Comes First – 2. The World of Harmony – 3. Harmony and Health – 4. The Spiritual Foundations of Medicine – 5. Respiration and Nutrition – 6. Respiration: I. The Effects of Respiration on Health – II. How to Melt into the Harmony of the Cosmos – 7. Nutrition on the Different Planes – 8. How to Become Tireless – 9. Cultivate an Attitude of Contentment.

226 – THE BOOK OF DIVINE MAGIC

1. The Danger of the Current Revival of Magic – 2. The Magic Circle of the Aura – 3. The Magic Wand – 4. The Magic Word – 5. Talismans – 6. Is Thirteen an Unlucky Number – 7. The Moon –8. Working with Nature Spirits – 9. Flowers and Perfumes – 10. We All Work Magic – 11. The Three Great Laws of Magic – 12. The Hand – 13. The Power of a Glance – 14. The Magical Power of Trust – 15. Love, the Only True Magic – 16. Never Look for Revenge –17. The Exorcism and Consecration of Objects – 18. Protect Your Dwelling Place.

227 – GOLDEN RULES FOR EVERYDAY LIFE

1. Life: our most precious possession – 2. Let your material life be consistent with your spiritual life – 3. Dedicate your life to a sublime goal – 4. Our daily life: a matter that must be transformed by the spirit – 5. Nutrition as Yoga – 6. Respiration – 7. How to recuperate energy – 8. Love makes us tireless – 9. Technical progress frees man for spiritual work – 10. Furnishing your inner dwelling – 11. The outer world is a

reflection of your inner world – 12. Make sure of a good future by the way you live today – 13. Live in the fullness of the present – 14. The importance of beginnings... etc.

228 – LOOKING INTO THE INVISIBLE
Intuition, Clairvoyance, Dreams

1. The Visible and the Invisible – 2. The Limited Vision of the Intellect, The Infinite Vision of Intuition – 3. The Entrance to the Invisible World: From Yesod to Tiphareth – 4. Clairvoyance: Activity and Receptivity – 5. Should We Consult Clairvoyants ? – 6. Love and Your Eyes Will be Opened – 7. Messages From Heaven – 8. Visible and Invisible Light: Svetlina and Videlina – 9. The Higher Degrees of Clairvoyance – 10. The Spiritual Eye – 11. To See God – 12. The True Magic Mirror: The Universal Soul – 13. Dream and Reality – 14. Sleep, an Image of Death – 15. Protect Yourself While You Are Asleep – 16. Astral Projection While Asleep – 17. Physical and Psychic Havens – 18. The Sources of Inspiration – 19. Sensation is Preferable to Vision.

229 – THE PATH OF SILENCE

1. Noise and Silence – 2. Achieving Inner Silence – 3. Leave Your Cares at the Door – 4. Make Your Meals an Exercise in Silence – 5. Silence, a Reservoir of Energies – 6. The Inhabitants of Silence – 7. Harmony, the Essential Condition for Inner Silence – 8. Silence, the Essential Condition for Thought – 9. The Quest for Silence is the Quest for the Centre – 10. Speech and the Logos – 11. A Master Speaks in Silence – 12. The Voice of Silence is the Voice of God – 13. The Revelations of a Starry Sky – 14. A Silent Room.

230 – THE BOOK OF REVELATIONS: A COMMENTARY

1. The Island of Patmos – 2. Introduction to the Book of Revelations – 3. Melchizedek and Initiation into the Mystery of the Two Principles – 4. Letters to the Church in Ephesus and Smyrna – 5. Letter to the Church in Pergamos – 6. Letter to the Church in Laodicea – 7. The Twenty-Four Elders and the Four Holy Living Creatures – 8. The Scroll and the Lamb – 9. The Hundred and Forty-Four Thousand Servants of God – 10. The Woman and the Dragon – 11. The Archangel Mikhaël Casts Out the Dragon – 12. The Dragon Spews Water at the Woman – 13. The Beast from the Sea and the Beast from the Land – 14. The Wedding Feast of the Lamb – 15. The Dragon is Bound for a Thousand Years – 16. The New Heaven and the New Earth –17. The Heavenly City.

231 – THE SEEDS OF HAPPINESS

1. Happiness: A Gift to be Cultivated – 2. Happiness is not Pleasure – 3. Happiness is Found in Work – 4. A Philosophy of Effort –5. Light Makes for Happiness – 6. The Meaning of Life – 7. Peace and Happiness – 8. If You want to be Happy, Be Alive – 9. Rise Above your Circumstances – 10. Develop a Sensitivity to the Divine – 11. The Land of Canaan – 12. The Spirit is Above the Laws of Fate – 13. Look for Happiness on a Higher Level – 14. The Quest for Happiness is a Quest for God – 15. No Happiness for Egoists – 16. Give Without Expecting Anything in Return – 17. Love Without Asking to be Loved in Return – 18. Our Enemies are Good for Us – 19. The Garden of Souls and Spirits – 20. Fusion on the Higher Planes – 21. We are the Artisans of Our Own Future.

232 – THE MYSTERIES OF FIRE AND WATER

1. The Two Principles of Creation, Water and Fire – 2. The Secret of Combustion – 3. Water, the Matrix of Life – 4. Civilization, a Product of Water – 5. The Living Chain of Sun, Earth and Water – 6. A Blacksmith Works with Fire – 7. Water is Born of Mountains – 8. Physical and Spiritual Water – 9. Feeding the Flame – 10. The Essential Role of Fire – 11. The Cycle of Water: Reincarnation –12. The Cycle of Water: Love and Wisdom – 13. A Candle Flame – 14. How to Light and Tend Fire – 15. Water, the Universal Medium – 16. The Magic Mirror – 17. Trees of Light – 18. The Coming of the Holy Spirit – 19. A Treasury of Pictures.

233 – YOUTH: CREATORS OF THE FUTURE

1. Youth, a World in Gestation – 2. The Foundation Stone of Life: Faith in a Creator – 3. A Sense of the Sacred – 4. The Voice of our Higher Nature – 5. Choosing the Right Direction – 6. Knowledge Cannot Give Meaning to Life – 7. Character Counts for More than Knowledge – 8. Learning to Handle Success and Failure – 9. Recognize the Aspirations of Soul and Spirit – 10. The Divine World, Our Own Inner World – 11. Did you Choose Your Own Family? –12. Benefit From the Experience of Older People – 13. Compare Yourself to Those Who Are Greater – 14. The Will Must be Sustained by Love – 15. Never Admit Defeat – 16. Never Give Way to Despair – 17. Artists of the Future – 18. Sexual Freedom – 19. Preserve the Poetry of Your Love – 20. Members of One Universal Family (I) (II).

234 – TRUTH: FRUIT OF WISDOM AND LOVE

1. The Quest for Truth – 2. Truth, the Child of Wisdom and Love – 3. Wisdom and Love; Light and Warmth – 4. The Love of a Disciple;

Alternation and Antagonism - The Law of Opposites – 8. 'To Work the Miracles of One Thing' - The Figure of Eight and the Cross – 9. The Caduceus of Hermes - The Astral Serpent – 10. *Iona*, Principle of Life - *Horeb*, Principle of Death – 11.The Triad *Kether-Chesed-Geburah* - Sceptre and Orb - Mind and Heart - A Straight Line and a Curved Line – 12. The Law of Exchange – 13. The Key and the Lock – 14.The Work of the Spirit on Matter - The Holy Grail – 15. Union of the Ego with the Physical Body – 16. The Sacrament of the Eucharist – 17.The Androgynes of Myth – 18. Union with the Universal Soul and the Cosmic Spirit.

Editor-Distributor

Editions PROSVETA S.A. - B.P. 12 - 83601 Fréjus Cedex (France)

Tel. 04 94 40 82 41 - Télécopie 04 94 40 80 05 - E-Mail: international@prosveta.com

Distributors

AUSTRALIA
QUEST, 484 Kent Street
2000 Sydney

AUSTRIA
HARMONIEQUELL VERSAND
A- 5302 Henndorf Hof 37
Tel and fax (43) 6214 7413

BELGIUM
PROSVETA BENELUX
Liersesteenweg 154 B-2547 Lint
Tel (32) 3/455 41 75 Fax 3/454 24 25
N.V. MAKLU Somersstraat 13-15
B-2000 Antwerpen
Tel. (32) 34 55 41 75
VANDER S.A.
Av. des Volontaires 321
B-1150 Bruxelles
Tel. (32) 27 62 98 04 Fax 27 62 06 62

BRAZIL
NOBEL SA – Rua da Balsa, 559
CEP 02910 - São Paulo, SP

BULGARIA
SVETOGLED
Bd Saborny 16 A appt 11 – 9000 Varna

CANADA
PROSVETA Inc. – 3950, Albert Mines
North Hatley (Qc), J0B 2C0
Tel. (819) 564-3287 Fax. (819) 564-1823
in Canada, call toll free: 1-800-584-8212
e-mail: prosveta@prosveta-canada.com

COLUMBIA
PROSVETA
Avenida 46 n° 19 - 14 (Palermo)
Santafe de Bogotá
Tel. (57) 232-01-36 – Fax (57) 633-58-03

CYPRUS
THE SOLAR CIVILISATION BOOKSHOP
73 D Kallipoleos Avenue - Lycavitos
P. O. Box 4947, 1355 – Nicosia
Tel: 02 377503 and 09 680854

GERMANY
PROSVETA Deutschland
Postfach 16 52 – 78616 Rottweil
Tel. 0741-46551 – Fax. 0741-46552
eMail: Prosveta.de@t-online.de
EDIS GmbH, Daimlerstr 5
82054 Sauerlach
Tel. (49) 8104-6677-0
Fax. (49) 8104-6677-99

GREAT BRITAIN
PROSVETA
The Doves Nest, Duddleswell Uckfield,
East Sussex TN 22 3JJ
Tel. (01825) 712988 - Fax (01825) 713386
E-Mail: prosveta@pavilion.co.uk

GREECE
EDITIONS PROSVETA – J. VAMVACAS
El. Venizelou 4 – 18531 - Athens

HOLLAND
STICHTING PROSVETA NEDERLAND
Zeestraat 50
2042 LC Zandvoort

HONG KONG
SWINDON BOOK CO LTD.
246 Deck 2, Ocean Terminal
Harbour City – Tsimshatsui, Kowloon

IRELAND
PROSVETA
The Doves Nest
Duddleswell Uckfield,
East Sussex TN 22 3JJ, U.K.

ITALY
PROSVETA Coop.
Casella Postale
06060 Moiano (PG)

LUXEMBOURG
PROSVETA BENELUX
Liersesteenweg 154 B-2547 Lint

NORWAY
PROSVETA NORDEN
Postboks 5101 – 1501 Moss

NEW ZEALAND
PSYCHIC BOOKS
p.o. Box 87-151
Meadowbank, Auckland 5

PORTUGAL
PUBLICAÇÕES
EUROPA-AMERICA Ltd
Est Lisboa-Sintra KM 14
2726 Mem Martins Codex

ROMANIA
ANTAR
Str. N. Constantinescu 10
Bloc 16A - sc A - Apt. 9
Sector 1 - 71253 Bucarest

SPAIN
ASOCIACIÓN PROSVETA ESPAÑOLA
C/ Ausias March n° 23 Ático
SP-08010 Barcelona
Tel (34) (3) 412 31 85 - Fax (3) 302 13 72

SWITZERLAND
PROSVETA
Société Coopérative
CH - 1808 Les Monts-de-Corsier
Tel. (41) 21 921 92 18
Fax. (41) 21 922 92 04
e-Mail: prosveta@swissonline.ch

UNITED STATES

PROSVETA USA, Inc.—P.O. Box 1176
New Smyrna Beach, FL 32170-1176
Web : www.prosveta-usa.com
E-mail : sales@prosveta-usa.com
VENEZUELA
Betty Munóz Urbanización Los Corales - avenida Principal
Quinta La Guarapa - LA GUAIRA - Municipio Vargas

PRINTED IN FRANCE IN AUGUST 1998
EDITIONS PROSVETA, Z.I. DU CAPITOU
B.P.12 – 83601 FRÉJUS
FRANCE

– N° d'impression: 2500 –
Dépôt légal: Août 1998
Printed in France